The Hardened Criminal

The Hardened Criminal

Folsom Prison Convicts

CELESTIAL ARTS
Millbrae, California

First Printing: February 1976
Made in the United States of America

Library of Congress Cataloging in Publication Data

Main entry under title:

The Hardened criminal.

CONTENTS: Jacobs, P. Prison:asset or liability?—
Lanners L.X.   Daily notes from a hiding place. —
Johnston, J. D.   Prison days.   [etc.]
    1.   Prisoners—California—Attitudes—Addresses,
essays, lectures.   2.   California. State Prison, Folsom
—Addresses, essays, lectures.
HV9475.C3F64   301.15′43′364   75-9077
ISBN 0-89087-070-5

1 2 3 4 5 6 7 8 − 80 79 78 77 76

CONTENTS

INTRODUCTION

At the time the idea for this book was born Ronald Reagan was Governor of California and the indeterminant sentence was in effect. Now Jerry Brown is Governor and release dates have been given to all prisoners who are due them. Still the day-to-day life of a convict in Folsom—or Attica, or San Quentin—goes on much as before.

A convict's day is built around small things that a "free" person takes for granted: Mail and visits—communication with the outside. The most significant impression received by one visiting inside the walls of Folsom, talking to the men in the yard, is the obsession these men have with communicating with the outside. Personal letters are of the gravest importance; an opportunity to talk face-to-face with someone from outside is a rare gift.

Originally the reason for publishing *The Hardened Criminal* was to facilitate communications, to allow "free" people an opportunity to hear these voices from within the walls, to overcome their sense of not being heard, of not being understood, of being forgotten. As the essays were written their substance became most important and the authors were encouraged to candidly express their feelings.

As a result the essays give a painfully real picture of what it is like to serve time in prison today. There is little time spent on the description of the prison, the cell, the facilities that are the tangible world of a convict. Instead the emphasis is on attitudes, hopes and desires, fears and frustrations.

The one element common to all the essays one to another is the anticipation of being free. However deeply they might dwell on the hopelessness of imprisonment they ultimately project ideas to a future day, a day without the gray walls.

An undertaking of this type requires the cooperation of many people who contribute to the success of the project without knowing exactly what the result will be. The Folsom Creative Writers' Workshop was the source of each of these essays; all the authors were members at one time or another. The members of the Workshop who did not participate in the anthology deserve special acknowledgment for their perseverance and contributions through the sessions that dealt solely with the book. Librarian Dean Gregory's sponsorship of the Workshop, his tacit approval and cooperation were necessary for the completion of the project. The many writers and others who have taken an interest in the Workshop and encouraged the work of its members, notably Max Schwartz, made the editing easy and virtually unnecessary.

CELESTIAL ARTS
Millbrae, California

CULT OF WARRIORS

Pancho Aguila

Nothing again. I'm losing touch. It's been months since I last heard from my family. Are they still there? They seem as phantoms in the dark recesses of my memory. I'm beginning to question their existence or their blood ties. The naivete of childhood formed an illusion of closeness. I was wrong. We are just another tragic scattering the system has produced . . . and I thought we were so close. I am envious of the kinship of the crime families of the East. They are like a ship sailing strong upon the battering seas, success-fully battling government and life—even death strengthens their ties. Maybe I am magnifying my plight and this is just one symptom of the social cancer of prison. Or maybe we are all stars separated by vast expanses of space. If our illu-mination dims do we become unnoticeable in the total brilliancy of being? You lose your luster in prison.

In the flow of days, months, years and events my letters have become inconsequential arrows against the omnipotent silence of exile. Its fiery breath has burned the networks of my communication to a crispy finale. My satellites of words and language have fallen, my temples are empty. My friends now walk the patrolled caverns of prison. The electric current feeding my television and radio are the fragile ties to life, open ears to the air waves full of radioed voices. I am reminded of a patient confined to an intensive-care ward wired with flowing blood lines and nutritional liquids in a gray world of subliminal survival.

Everyday is a stone block blotting out the world of the streets. My stone blocks now number into the thousands and the thickness and heights of the wall take their toll. Now, they are the physical qualities of alienation. The other side of the walls is intangible, an illusive ghost, but nonetheless gnawing at the heart. The energy of alienation transmutes into the Einsteinian matter of "prison exile." The differences of alienation is only a question of the physical state on either side of the wall. This pervasive state of affairs is as American as apple pie, as a contemporary convicted revolutionary once said of violence.

Every passing day I realize that the prison-universe is a fabricated reality. We are like a computer fed data which leads us to certain patterns of thought reminiscent of a chain-of-prisoners being lead before a judge and playing a judicial game of behaviors. We are like an outside casing going down a conveyor belt, painted and sprayed with systematic colors to change the way we appear to others, but our insides are of an opposite passion. The questions of life have meaning and we search deeply to attain the light and purpose to live.

This is a separate world. The prison is a separate reality. We are the shadows of Plato's dialogue dancing in the darkened cave, a tiny stream of sun casting our lives on the stone walls. We are the ones that disappear behind the high walls for years, decades, a lifetime for many, to eventually rise from the living death. A convict-novelist described us as "No beast so fierce" correctly capturing, I think, the spirit of men released or escaped. I have felt this cyclonic spirit of savage defiance, crude and fomenting in its primitiveness. The jungle has not left us.

The perennial outlaw is forever doing battle with the state. Western religion would have us believe the eternal forces of evil and good are daily enacting their deadly drama on the stage of the world. Others believe the class struggle of the powerless vs. the powerful is the real issue that brings the violence and war to our midst. Being an admitted institutional irreligionist, branded by the contemporary government an *official criminal,* regarded as and referred to as a hoodlum by my keepers, my preferences of views gravitate towards the rational of class-war, not by strict choice but as the circumstances of life would have it.

This line of thought will lead us logically to question, philosophically, the concept of the criminal or what theoretically I am supposed to be by American social standards.

Criminal in the dictionary is defined as implying wickedness, and one who commits crime which are offenses against the social order and existing morality. Generally, all you will find is this very basic, terse definition.

A *criminal,* without question, is a loser, but not in the absolute for it can be argued that a stretch in the pen is just a battle lost in a warring life. When you find yourself in a cage encircled by heavily armed gun towers on high thick surrounding stone walls, patrolled and commanded by a phalanx of hardened guards, it is exceedingly difficult to convince yourself, or any other, that you have not lost in the social game of life. The only spiritual salvation is the patriotic exhortation "I have just begun to fight" or, more prosaically, "there'll be another day."

Accepting the fact of confinement is more a process of osmosis or that of a gentle psychic murder. Life is actually killed or we are left with a tragic resemblance of it. Coming to grips with reality and enduring the prison of bars, guns, hostilities and fears we become a strange product of men, childish at times and frightfully brutal and indifferent at others. Sentimentally caressing the cats that have made this old prison fortress a home while thinking of devious bloodletting fates for rat-informers or for that stranger we have grown to hate without rhyme or reason—even genocide of whole races are entertained in casual friendly conversations. If hatred had density and weight we surely would sink and disappear into the infernal regions of Poe's "House of Usher," but I'm not saying hate is purely a negative emotion for it can be the will to power, a superhuman agency that leads us to action and energy to whatever path we choose. All the above scribbling, pounds and breathes in my very veins and blood. I am immersed in this reality.

In this cesspool of fantastic, irrational madness we come to observe the nature of man in prison and, possibly, the nature of humanity in general, if we are pessimistic. Any man (or woman) of normal intelligence who observes the psychology of the "joint" firsthand, no doubt will be confused and shocked by what he sees and hears, but the greater bewilderment to an objective observer will be that this same sensitive, intelligent prisoner will be a maker of confusion and shock given a set of circumstances that can and do arise. A comedy of errors can turn into a tragedy of mistakes often violent and final. This is a crazy place. Madness! Every word, every look can be dangerous and as serious as a heart attack when tension gets so thick it can be cut with a knife and ironically, but understandably, politeness and courtesy is quick and emphatic. A world of contradictions are the big houses of America.

But what of the quality of life in these human zoos, these surrealistic warehouses of human beings? How does one cope in a captive mechanical environment of concrete and steel, devoid of even the privilege of viewing the stars, the face of the moon and the even harsher anti-human separation and exile from the understanding folds of our loved ones? I wish I could make these words come alive with the clank of slamming bars and make you feel the iciness of the cement walls of the cell.

I think the real drama of prison is the inner reality and interior life of the captive, as is true of all human experience. I can describe the mechanical operations of a prison, the systematic bureaucratic treadmill, the schedule, the routines and policy, but all I will have done is separate the bones from the frame and you will have missed the essence, the life, the quality of the subject. This essence behind the mask of prison, the inner core of the outer shell, this internal body is what I wish to describe. For we are all part of the great soul of life in the concentrated chambers and social pressure cooker of contemporary America, and to know one is to know all.

What is the gamut of emotions that a man or woman feels whose life is relegated, two-thirds of the 24-hour life cycle, to a cage? Are they sheep or tigers? What of the violence?

Hate, despair, frustration, bitterness, defeat are the wheels of the demon-sled that leads us into violence. There is no presumption in these writings that violence is necessarily an abhorrent, deviant behavior characteristic of biblical anti-Jesus characters and hordes. Violence can be a medicine to the ailing of oppression, giving needed cathartic release by providing outlets for the bitter waters that flow within . . . the only difficulty is that these holes of liberation can attain the stature of stab wounds or bullet penetrations depending on the degrees of aggressiveness released. I am not questioning the morality of right or wrong, for when certain meteorological factors consummate the clouds will tear in rain. Whether an Attica, a prison rape or a stabbing over cigarettes, these actions are products of a machinery dealing with the oppression and mutilation of the mental life. The constitutional protections of cruel and unusual punishment seem too mild to capture this reality. If you think this an extreme theorization one has only to consider the bloody last four years of prison revolts, internal prison wars and carnage, the numerous suicides and overdoses that seldom make sensational headlines. These are items aside from the long-term investments of this so-called correction system that produces those "no beast so fierce."

[The prisons have become a breeding ground, a training ground for a cult of warriors.] Apart from the establishment's military there is no institution than that of prison where martial qualities and characteristics are so admired and emulated. These cages will make a strong soldier out of you or else the disgust of the yard . . . a rat collaborator, a vegetable (psycho, stone crazy) or a taking-it-in-the-ass punk (as one homosexual I know refers to himself). In fact, I believe this destructive energy, a Frankenstein, a dragon, ultimately will be part of the creative force responsible for the new upcoming social order. Hate, despair, frustration, bitterness, defeat . . . these wholesale national products may very well be the dark clouds of the tempest before the dawn.

The duality of phenomena even extends to the emotional state of the captives of the modern 20th century dungeons of America. On the plus side of the emotional character of the captive we have hope, faith, patience, strength and imagination. To survive the long ordeal of these cages and keep our self-dignity we have to incorporate the above virtues as graduation requisites of this university of hardknocks.

No matter the length of time we have been locked down or the stretch of dead years that has been programmed for us to serve, we all entertain a concept, however vague, of what we desire when we hit the bricks (return to the streets). This concept may be an everchanging fantasy, a freestyle flow of indecision originating with the insecure knowledge of having to serve an incomprehensible and repulsive life sentence . . . as incomprehensible as mentally grasping the difference between a billion and a million objects.

Our dream can be an objective having such a vivid reality in our mind that we feel it ready to break out into the world at any opportune time. We know that time is sure to come, and often having a quality so real that we see it taking on physical qualities all around us. These dreams and hopes are our savior, without them the suicide rope reaches out with its icy twines—perhaps as a legitimate defense mechanism to our unnatural adversity.

In the endless stretch of these empty suns and hollow moons, in the lonely holes of our being, it is our dreams that are nurtured, our hopes that are crystallizing, that will carry us to other dimensions where the birds sing freely and the stars light the night joyously. This will be the supreme day of our freedom when we are reborn to the real world of life beyond the gun tower walls of power and oppression. You can never kill the spirit of warriors, only cage them. If you are in the business of squashing and stomping out the tide of rebellion it would be far wiser to contemplate the causes of disturbances and disturbers.

I feel there are objective mechanics which have subjectively influenced my life as it has others at the same time. When power and wealth is controlled, monopolized and stratified, those at the bottom will seek to reach the top as surely as some will weep and cry at the bottom landings. If the world and history is ever to change the structure of American economics must collapse. The giant circus tents must fall to the ground. Broadly speaking (poetically), a giant summit meeting of an entire human race must agree to share the treasures of earth, taking example from the sun who generously and abundantly showers heat to all revolving territories and faces of this our planet Earth. From a restricted cage to an infinitely expanding universe, the underlying energy and force of life is the reach for freedom, for growth, I am guilty of this crime! We are guilty! Guilty! Guilty!

INMATE, OUTMATE

Saul Paul Austin

The spark igniting this harangue is an article by Dr. Robert M. Linder that appeared in the *folsom flash*, entitled "Mind of the Inmate," wherein he very aptly describes prisoners as: "From the moment the offender is turned over to the guard at the gate, he lives in a dream . . . [world of reality]."

The truth is that the majority of inmates do not live in a dream world—but some do. And it is the few that Linder has chosen for stereotyping the many. In any event, the Doctor's tones conform to the generally held opinion that the inmate's destiny is fully beyond his control, and I resent that. So it is that what follows herein is based on my observations of people in prison during the year I've spent inside awaiting a ruling on my appeal, and of the people who keep them there, and of the people who send them there. I'm not writing herein to either win friends or to kowtow to people, but rather to instruct, to uplift, to edify. As a composer of first-rate fiction (honest!), I've learned to objectively observe and interpret people and

17

events; thus it is that I have sketched my observations, etched out pragmatic and viable insights.

What does society owe the convicted criminal anyway—if anything at all? Conversely, what does he owe society, his victim? Or, for that matter, does he even give a damn about society? What causes violent behavior in the prisons, and how does the inmate spend his time, can he be rehabilitated and *must* prison be a liability? And who has the greater I.Q., the inmate, or the outmate (i.e. society)?

Consider this: I once announced to twenty members of the prison Gavel Club that "I am resigning my post as Parliamentarian, but will otherwise retain my membership." I made the said announcement loudly . . . clearly. Yet, during the interim of the following weekly meeting I was approached by no less than twelve members expressing regret that I had "resigned from the *Gavel Club*"! Moreover, even though I'd explained the true facts of the thing to them at the time of their inquiries, they were stunned to see me at the following meeting! Fortunately for me I'd written out and submitted my statements concerning resignation to the secretary. But to me, a novice, the incident set off an alarm, partially so because I'd expected to find that inmates would be more observant as a result of the life-styles they lead, I had reasoned that it sharpened their wits to have to constantly live by them; they also have time in which to think and formulate things. Be that as it may, I began asking well-chosen people to tell me, without giving names or specific details, how many people are rumored to have been "shanked" (knifed) because one inmate had not understood another's words. Some of the answers I got were probably the wildest of speculation but the results were nonetheless impressive. So perhaps there is evidence here that inmates are living in a dreamlike state, and it is this very same existence that renders the victim of a stabbing so vulnerable; for it is not an easy task to stalk and kill a healthy, alert person; wound him, perhaps, but *killing* with a knife isn't the easiest thing in the world to do in the first place. Even so, we must bear in mind that those inmates who are involved in such carryings on are not the majority of the prison population, and even if they are living in a dreamlike state that doesn't mean that the majority is doing so, as the good Doctor has said they are. I suppose that, in addition to overcrowding, one of the main causes of violence in prison, especially among young, energetic inmates, is a lack of exercise, which causes body tensions to mount, explode in uncontrollable, violent behavior. But at the base of all this—at least from my coign of vantage—is the fact that most inmates think of violence a lot, and they don't think so much in terms of doing it as they do in terms of it being done to them. Thus we must conclude that things are not so terribly different in prison than out, in the sense that a handful of terrorists can and do communicate their violence to large numbers of people who're not directly involved in the initial act.

In any event, the Gavel Club incident is indicative of something bigger, something much more bizarre: the mean educational level of both inmates and outmates is declining; objective reading, listening, and interpretation are becoming alarmingly scarce (thanks to the advent of such things as television, which rob the individual of his need to think). Further, if race is a factor in it, the whites are the hardest hit by the decline in intelligence (can anyone explain the bungling of Watergate and the votes that made it possible?).

But in spite of that, if the most ignorant people in any given society are its dregs and if dregs for the most part concentrate themselves on the bottom, then there is no doubt that prison is society's bottom, teeming with the criminally ignorant; that is, the older a man becomes the less likely he is to do ignorantly violent things, a fact well illustrated by the comparatively low rate of violent incidents among the men in Folsom—the youngest man here is approximately 24—but conversely, a vast number of younger inmates act through emotion rather than reason.

They'll gladly stab each other over a carton of cigarettes, or over some abstract honor or principle that they never had in the first place. Moreover—whether justified or not—they feel that certain discriminatory traits inherent in society has forced them into crime as a means of decent survival. And the only remorse I've heard expressed over or in relation to a crime was that the inmate regretted either having been too lenient with his victim or having employed too little cunning in the perpetration of his crime. Moreover, a bit of very careful observation has convinced me that not only inmates but Americans generally lack the capacity for *true* remorse. A few have it, but most don't. The majority feel remorse but it's because their own personal plans didn't work out—not because they offended or hurt someone else. Oh, we like to think that they feel *true* remorse, but they don't.

On the other side of the bars, society neither condones nor forgives the criminal, they could care less whether he feels remorse or not, there is no sympathy, no one questions whether or not he's guilty or innocent, there is little concern for his welfare, society could care less about winning his trust or potentially productive cooperation; and therefore, inmate and outmate are mutually exclusive, mutually unyielding in their ignorance—and American Democracy is dying.

Indeed, it seems to me that someplace along the line we've all forgotten how to examine ourselves for culpability. We've all removed the I-was-wrong clause from our personal lexicons, and we've forgotten that when everybody's right—everyone's wrong. Anarchy? Is that where we're headed? *No conscience, no recourse to law,* was our primordial state, remember? Is mankind progressing? But perhaps there is some middle ground of salvation. Come, let us seek after it!

The typical inmate posits that "society won't help me and they won't let me help myself," while society discreetly hides its face in apathy and vindictiveness. This destructive attitude of the latter carries over into his personal life, affecting the quality of life throughout his community and, ultimately, throughout his nation. Paradoxically—and I won't attempt interpretation of their motives—inmates exhibit a startlingly keen interest in community events. They displayed real concern over the plight of Biafra and Honduras, and their shocked dismay over Watergate amazed me; as though they thought there was virtue in politics! Nonetheless, construing one's life around the won't-let-me-help-myself bit is an attitude that likewise spills over into the penal community and beyond, affecting the national quality of life and contributing to the dreamlike existence theory, because to suggest that one is helpless is an open invitation to relax, and relaxation brings sleep, and sleep begets dreaming of the sort mentioned by the Doctor. Moreover, the so-called helpless bit begs contrasting the relatively leisurely life in prison against the hectic pace of wage slaves: they rarely ever find the time in which to read a good book, much less time for seriously studying to better their lot.

Paradoxically again, there are lots of inmates who do have the time, yet not really knowing what they want out of life and lacking the motivation, discipline, etcetera, to go after it if they did know, they blindly volunteer themselves for stale working-class principles that, in many cases, have no bearing whatever on impressing the parole authority, no relevance to the life they'll be called on to deal with beyond the bars. And so, clinging tenaciously to their menial tasks, dreaming of some mirage called *rehabilitation*, exercising their bodies at the expense of their fallow minds, they grimace otiosely as Father Time goes marching by. Alternatively, consider how prison served O. Henry, Ernest Toller, Nehru, Anwar Sadat, and even Hitler. Eugene Debs campaigned for the presidency from a jail cell, and Mohammed returned from his desert exile with the renewed vitality that nearly imposed Islam on the entire globe. Still, some inmates are gobbling up poisoned apples of the genre handed out by Dr. Linder. They consume the fruit and sleep again. But theirs is the troubled sleep, for it robs them of their self-reliance, the less they seek their own salvation—the only *true* salvation—by realistically redefining their goals and priorities.

As for living in a dream world of unreality, the man who sleeps in prison is a fool, the man who encourages him to sleep is a criminal, and the man who wakes him is liable to get killed. During my childhood I was taught that "education makes us easy to lead but hard to guide, easy to govern but impossible to enslave"; and this is analogously relevant in the sense that regardless the servitude of the body the intelligent mind not only remains free but continues to grow as well. But *ignorance* is ruling the bower of both inmate and outmate alike, leading me to say without reservation that it is the most lethal foe stalking democracy today. It breeds the murder in prison and the apathy outside. When it is compounded by unsalutary brainwashing there is bound to be trouble. Some inmates have been completely brainwashed and institutionalized, which means that they regard prison as an end rather than a means, utilize freedom only as their vehicle to recidivism. Not even the freedom from bindings of the wage slave is utilized in meditating and widening vistas of freedom but are rather squandered in such as inane conversations about goodtimes had in some previous prison. They do not contrast freedom and imprisonment but rather they contrast one degree of imprisonment against another: they do not say, "The steaks at Hyatt House are better than those served in prison"; but rather they say, "The steaks served in San Quentin are better than those served in Vacaville"—their entire frame of reference is therefore intraprisonal. (Me? When I'm fortunate enough to get a steak I forget all about the possibility that there might be one better across town someplace, I just thank the Lord and concentrate all my undivided attention on the one I see.)

Further, those who've been brainwashed speak of freedom only as some vague abstract, perfunctorily, as if giving lip service to a desire for freedom is a duty that must be performed alternative to being declared abnormal by their peers. Thus it is that what worked for Malcolm X., O. Henry, etcetera, is out of the grasp of the brainwashed and the institutionalized. But there are people in prison who are preparing for the future, making themselves ready for life on the outside by attending the various educational programs offered in prison. There is one hell of a shortage of tradeschool facilities, but the really determined people are not using that as an excuse to sleep. They study their text books, they know that they can get grants to attend the schools after they're out of prison. There are also people who don't like to go to school because for one reason or another they can't function in a classroom atmosphere. But they keep busy in their cells, studying on their own, doing artwork, hobbies, crafts, etcetera. But they do not sleep. Thus it is that in prison as on the outside one man's meat is poison for another. One man grows, thriving on the very conditions that are destroying another, one man's cell is a tomb, the cell next door is a manger, to one man prison is a mortal death, to another it is but the death of the Phoenix. Moreover, just as it is true that many outmates are failures by nature, so must society realize and deal with the fact that all prisoners are not rehabilitatable and therefrom concentrate all society's best efforts on saving those still within the pale of redemption. The incorrigibles should be punished as quickly and as mercifully as possible and released.

What is "rehabilitation" anyway? A better way to say it would be, "open his eyes to his potential"; and thus the term "salvageable" might easily supplant the term "rehabilitatable," because it is more practical. The term rehabilitate means to restore some person or thing to its original *good* or *excellent* condition or state. Very obviously then, if a person was brought up in the slums, stealing and killing to stay alive, we don't want to restore him to his original *good* state prior to releasing him from prison.

Hey!—what's all this hub-bub about rehabilitation and the so-called scientific exploration of it anyway? It is no secret that if a man needs enough money or self-fulfillment, or both, to live on terms with himself in the world he will not be so-called rehabilitated until he has what he must. If a man is imprisoned for theft and while in prison he becomes a selling author, earning the monies implied, it is then safe to assume his so-called rehabilitation. Likewise, it is no secret that if a man is serving his third term for rape and rape is the only crime he's ever committed, and if he somehow gets his genitals cut off, then he has been rehabilitated and should be released forthwith! By my fiat, I swear it! No mystery, no likely in-between. So it is that as usual the public is being taken for the customary multi-billion-dollar ride on the malarkey-train of rehabilitation—the just fruits of outmate apathy? Hey, you take away the tax monies that line avaricious pockets and within a year you won't be able to find the word "rehabilitation" even in the *Oxford English Dictionary*, nor a petty criminal in prison.

But how do we know who can be "salvaged" and who cannot? Truth is, we don't. It is entirely possible that a man will spend forty years in and out of prison, then suddenly do an irrevocable about-face on crime. Obversely, it is equally possible that a man may never be arrested until age forty, and that afterward he will never once turn either his head or hand away from crime. Yet the guidelines for detecting the salvageable are so elementary as to be negligible. But as we get into that let me point out the two major divisions of ignorance: noxiously ignorant and innoxiously ignorant. The latter types are not likely to go to prison but often prove so irksome to their employers and friends that . . . if wishing would make it so . . .? But it is the criminal ignorance which breeds blindly unreasoning contempt for both extant and aborning healthy conventions, contempt for the rescuing hand, for other inmates, and for society in general: the dreggiest of the dregs, men who can't be civilized and don't want to be. Via determining who is salvageable and who is not, I posit that society should operate in a manner of cooperation with the criminal, beginning from the time of his first arrest, that things can eventually reach the point that society can say with a perfectly good conscience, "Hey, we don't care anymore. We've given you X-number of breaks, you had a good income and a good life on the outside. But *yuh* blew it. Well, from here on in, my fine-feathered friend, it's punishment, pure and simple—we're no longer out to salvage the mess you've made of your life. You're noxiously ignorant."

I further posit that it should be made possible for those inmates who have something in common to be in a prison facility together—on a voluntary basis of course. Just as the outmates do it. One of the most sickening sights I've seen was a little inmate proudly beaming that he'd been in and out of prison for twenty years. He actually thought he was entitled to respect for that, his éclat, he wanted to be hero-worshipped. For the person who takes pride in being in prison, the person who has actually reached the point that he thinks prison is the right place to be, regards it as "my team," brags about it as though it were his favorite alma mater, for this type person, it is already too late, much too late; and he'll probably have a negative influence on those who are forced by extant circumstances to associate with him. Sure, we as prisoners have but pitifully few rights and even those few must be constantly defended. But we also have the right—even the obligation—to not become so involved in defending that we forget it's wrong to be here in the first place. But the fact is that some inmates want deeper into the criminal community while others want out—all the way; each group should be allowed the pursuit of happiness without interference from the other. The close quarters, the tendencies of the obtuse to proliferate racism, the facetiousness, the tendencies of the illiterate to cause trouble over such trivialities as others would scoff at; these factors and more render this voluntary-basis thing all the more desirable and practical in prison. Moreover, the statisticians tell us repeatedly that the recidivism rate among high-school graduates is extremely low, and this fact alone stands as a mighty testimonial to the potential of the common-interest posit.

As for the apathy of outmates, they might mark well that we are in the rudiments of drastic changes in the quality of American life. Historically, such upheavals usually presage unpredictable behavior of the undesirable sort in people who under normal circumstances are law-abiding. Moreover, due to the provocative examples being set by our national leaders, more and more outmates will be turning to crime until such time as the country is going smoothly again and all the shock waves have been absorbed by time and good behavior. I believe that the fact that Americans made such a poor showing at the polling places in the immediate aftermath of Watergate is as good an indicator of this as any. And so outmates today may well be inmates tomorrow. Many—like Nixon, who nearly found himself face-to-face with the vindictive law-and-order he preached—had best beware lest they find themselves victims of their apathy to the handling of lawbreakers.

We are not at sixes and sevens over what the public can do if it has a mind to, or over what the inmate can do to save himself, for in either instance the change must come first inside the individual; after that the possibilities are limitless. Ever and anon those inmates who are awake should ask themselves "what do I want from life and is what I'm doing while in prison related in any way to what I plan to do when I'm out?" If the thing he or she is doing has no bearing on the future goals one has set for oneself it's a waste of time, and the person had best become relevant or risk a return to prison.

But it is chiefly to the outmate that I address myself, for they have the power of freedom. They must begin by reevaluating themselves, the nation, and the inmate; for vengeance and apathy (the knife blade along which they're crawling) are two-way streets: in the days ahead you'll be literally paying for those luxuries with the bread off your tables. That is, paying more tax monies to confine petty criminals than they have either the imagination or the ambition to steal (I know a man who is spending two costly years in here on your expense account for stealing a thirty-dollar lawn mower). If society is no more yielding or merciful in its posture than the criminal, then society is his peer. The man standing on the gallows with the rope knotted about his neck cannot be called upon to grant the hangman mercy. Like it or not, the onus is on society. Sure, you've suffered at the hands of government's contumely; but whose fault was that anyway? Could it be that you were too trusting, too quick to ignore, too ready to reject the facts when they were presented to you and too adept at labeling the prophets "loonies" when they came to warn you? Could it be that the politicians somehow got the impression that your intelligence is so low now that there is no longer the need to bother keeping up the pretense of respecting it, and that they have now embarked on a new policy of openly treating you on the level of intelligence suggested by your inaction, misaction, and apathy to the corruption in government? If so, what could you do to stop them? Oh, I'm all too aware that bitterness rules the bower, no one believes in the polls anymore because everyone is aware that even there he is being manipulated, not really making a decision for himself. But thou shalt not cry craven, thou willst not despond in adversity, thou shan't retreat. Thou must retrieve thy wounded pride, dust it off, get right back out there and get to closing the loopholes that thou shouldst not have left open in the first place. It all began with the small evils, such as ignoring the plight of convicts, did it not?

Consider this: very recently the media carried the story of an inmate who—having been kept at your expense for thirteen trouble-free years—upon appearing before the parole board was refused a release for no other reason than that he had no blemish (had been in no trouble) on his record. Did you know that? The indefinite sentence must be abolished. But meantime you must demand that these petty monarchs and psychopaths who reign over the parole hearings be photographed and televised by the media; personally exposed to and questioned by the public whose intelligence they're insulting by wasting lives and money. Why isn't this being done already? We do it to our president, are these Rhadamanthines something special? Have you seen a parole board member on TV explaining why he made a decision? Was it not petty abuses such as these, such as the tolerating of abuse of individuals and minorities that the great seditionists from the Rhineland looked at in gaging the naked pathway, to American Democracy through the Watergate, etcetera? Doesn't anyone care about the Laws of Relativity anymore? When Ford declares that he is "a carbon copy of Nixon" that is the thing we're supposed to act on; when someone speaks out in support of the enemies of democracy as did Tricia, Reagan, etcetera, they are either (a) ignorant, or (b) criminally insane, or (c) birds of the same feather as the usurper. If they fit into the first two categories they've no business in public affairs, if in the third they belong in jail for treason. If they claim "loyalty," familial or otherwise, they must be made to understand that this too is a crime because we are not seeking to establish a tribalism here but rather to maintain our democracy. In short, if we do not want the lice we must stop the bloody nits.

In summation, Eris and Loki are tossing our government back and forth in a deadly game of catch today. And if our regaining control is consequent upon our perception of detail, then we must perceive that the totality of our existence is calculable in terms of assets and liabilities and that intelligence dictates that we must cut our losses and let our profits run. There is no doubt in my mind that the American people are basically winners; that we must face an uncertain future together is nothing new, but as we do so I can think of no people with whom I'd rather stand, and no people in whom I see a greater profit. Afterall, does not the flower smell more fragrant when stepped on?

LETTERS

Charles Butler

Letters have held a secure niche in literature and communications from the time men began to transcribe their thoughts into written characters for communicating thoughts and ideas, through the times of biblical "chronicals" and "letters" written by the apostles typified by Paul's letters to the Corinthians. This secured position remained inviolate up and through the age of the great philosophers, sages, poets of later times.

In this century it is said, and the facts seem to support it, that personal communications through letters are fast becoming a thing of the past. The advent of modern communications—the telephone, teletype, satellite relays—continues to hasten the demise of the letter as a convenient form of personal communication.

The most notable exception to this decline may be found in prisons. Men and women in prisons all over the world find that letters are sometimes their only contact with the "outside," since the letter represents the least threat to the security of the detaining facility.

To them then, letters are often the one link, the one psychic emotional lifeline, with the larger reality, the society that imprisons them. Being emotionally emasculated and physically separated from their societal roots can be a fate worse than death.

The letters you're about to read fall into roughly four categories. They mirror my pain, anger, frustrations, sadness, as well as the rare moments of joy and exhilaration. They may at times appear pretentious, selfish, emotional and almost irrational, but they represent *me* at my most happy, anguished, and unguarded moments.

Category number one may be best described as "first contact" letters. They're characterized by a desperation, an urgent anguished reaching out, reaching for friendship and concern that might dispel the terrible feeling of isolation. . . of being forgotten, and finally succeeding.

Category number two is an attempt to mend family ties that had been lost over a period of 17 years, specifically with my brother Neil and three other relatives, sisters and brothers . . . the only surviving "family." The letters speak more precisely for themselves. Category three is a letter to the mother of someone very dear to me, a girlfriend that I wanted very much to be more than a girlfriend. I needed the trust and confidence of her mother, to overcome the stigma of being forever rejected for being in prison. It, too, makes its own statement.

Finally, category four is a happy, jiving, bullshitting letter with a very, very close friend with whom I enjoy a down-to-earth, confident relationship. Together they give an accurate picture of me, not necessarily flattering, but the essential me, nonetheless. Read them. Laugh, cry, make of them what you will . . . but read them!

Dear Amy:

Here is my second letter to you, dear friend. I hope the "intensity" of my last letter didn't turn you off! It's just that I was so happy . . . so excited, so flattered that you liked my work, that you were impressed enough to write me, that I now have a beautiful, sensitive person to write to!

Your letter was at once an affirmation, and a ray of sunshine into my little corner. It helped to dispel some of the terrible loneliness and dark despair that lurks in every minute, every hour, every day and night of my confinement.

You seem to be a sensitive, kind, gentle person—a person with a lot of love, compassion, and goodness in your heart for your fellow man! Encountering such a person restores my faith in mankind. And it leaves me terribly excited, and wanting to get to know that person better— can you dig where I'm coming from?

I must confess, I have not known much love in my life. I've learned to love only through bitter heartbreak, pain, and adversity; realizing that men and women must come together or be destroyed by their own fears and hatred. Hatred has a way of consuming the hater.

Oh wow, I too am a "people observer." They're an endless source of fascination, and fun to be with, at least some of them! But even for the exceptions, I think I still love them.

You said you weren't sure of what profession you'd like to get into. Whatever you eventually decide, dear friend/sister, I'd like to "stand" by you, in a manner of speaking. That is, helping you if you desire and I can, with advice, caring, sharing and exchanging. You can help me also. You can help me to feel human . . . to feel concerned and cared for, to be a good friend. You can help me to not feel forgotten! You can help me by writing to me often . . . exchanging good feelings, ideas, viewpoints, writings. I'd very much like to see excerpts from some of your novels, or anything else you've written. But, enough "seriousness"! Yea, yea, you said you play the guitar. Heavy!! I play a pretty mellow harmonica, I'm told. I play both blues harmonica, and mellower stuff! Never coordinated it with dramatic, inspirational readings though. Hey, I've got to try that! Probably be a neat thing to do. I can get it on with a guitar too, but my musical talent seems to center on the harmonica. A friend of mine taught me a lot about rhythms, lyrics, etc. The blues influence comes from my living two doors from a bluesman of some note in San Francisco. He and I use to jam in his accoustically tight and soundproof basement.

But, my number 1 love is writing!! It's such a neat way of expressing things and there's a sort of "permanence" about it, dig? Developing your style until you're able to capture essences, learning to write eloquently so as to pinpoint and address, and expose all the suffering, pain, and degradation around us! To encourage, exhort, stimulate people to be more sensitive and loving toward each other.

Talking about you getting into my writing, I really got into your letter, dear sister! What an incredibly beautiful, mind-blowing gesture that was! Please don't stop writing to me. I hope your father doesn't mind. Got to close this before I talk your head off! You'd better not try to respond to this letter on every point, you know, it being so long. Just write naturally, and pick the points you want to respond to. *Please* write soon!

Peace & Love,
Charles

P.S. As soon as I hear from you we'll start exchanging writings.

Dear Sharon:

Oh wow, was I really *surprised* and *happy* to get your letter my friend!? It's an incredibly good feeling and it did neat things for my head! I also breathed a sigh of relief that you weren't put off by that totally unexpected letter from a complete stranger! I got your name and address from a mutual friend. Yes indeed, that goes a long ways in restoring my faith in mankind! In order to appreciate the exquisite feeling you'd have to understand how incredibly lonely and abandoned I felt. Thanks a lot for the very warm and human response!

We seem to have more in common music-wise so I'll talk about that first. If I had to describe my musical taste, I'd say I like straight ahead, laid back, hard-driving music with lots of guitar. Of course, this is not a hard, fast thing. In certain moods I like soft, mellow stuff. Have you heard Clapton's "461 Ocean Boulevard"? Oh wow, I hope you'll forgive my excitement and exuberance, it's just that I feel so good about having a friend to write to!!! Hey, I'm listening to "Lucy in the Sky with Diamonds" right now over the prison radio! What I mean is each cell has a headset where each inmate can hear music over a radio located in a central location.

Ah, but enough music for now! I'd very much like to know more about you: Are you going to college? Something about yourself, Alturas, or whatever! Oh, before I forget it, would it be asking too much to get a picture of you? You see, I threw the paper away with your picture in it, when it looked as if you weren't going to answer my letter! Your face has already become sort of, how shall I say, hazy in my mind! I'll be happy to send you one of me, but it may take awhile, 'cause being in prison causes some complications, know what I mean? I think I might be able to eventually get some made.

Incidentally, my "home," such as it was, is San Francisco. I'm not sure where I'll take up residence when I get out, things are so uncertain! Just in case you're curious, Folsom is just a stone's throw from Sacramento, and it's an incredibly stark, imposing sight! It's an old, old prison built in the early 1800s and is just barely fit for human habitation. It's cold, very cold, in the winter, and very hot in the summer.

Needless to say, prison life is, or can be, very brutal. We have all types of men locked up here, from petty, relatively minor offenders to very serious offenders. The human waste and degradation is awesome! Men survive this experience unscarred . . . if they're tough and determined! Others are less strong and don't do so well. There are pimps, petty thieves, fallen aristocrats, sexual deviates, burglars, robbers, murderers and, this is important, men so normal that their imprisonment almost constitutes a crime in itself! There are men here who engage in homosexual acts with other men, there are men here that made only one mistake and found themselves in prison, and are basically good men at heart!

Having you as a pen pal to write me is probably the best thing that's happened in a long, long time! I want to impress upon you that your letters will be appreciated, very much indeed, and I will maintain everything we say in our letters in the strictest confidence! Feel free to talk about absolutely anything, or ask any question regardless how sensitive it may seem. I've lost most of my shyness and thin-skinned nature since I've come to prison! I'm certainly going to be telling you things in confidence, and I will be very direct because friends should be able to confide in one another, right? So, whether it be life in prison, politics, music, world affairs, the type of sex life men in prison have, or whatever, feel free to talk about it with me, OK? I think the essence of friendship is being able to confide in, and talk about anything without being self-conscious! Ah yes, the reason I'm making this letter so long is that I want to give you a sort of picture and a basis on which to build our correspondence. Don't feel obligated to respond to every point in this letter . . . we've got plenty of time to do that in future letters. Oh yes, if you have any *specific* questions that you'd like to direct to a thing or area, by all means do so!

I've really got to cut this short before I write you a book!! I hope you understand that it's my excitement. One final thing, you have made me a *very* happy person by agreeing to be a friend and pen pal! Gotta go. Take care and please write as soon as you possibly can. Keep smilin'! Peace!

Love & Brotherhood
Charles

Dear Wally:

It was really great to get your letter, man! It makes me feel so much better knowing that I now have a good friend to rap and relate to. As ordinary as that last sentence sounds, I really and truly mean it, brother! It's from the bottom of my heart!

Judging from your letter, we have a few other things in common as well as the common need to communicate. I too tend to *not* fit into "groups" that always seem somehow to end up being elitist, exclusive, and "apart" from the mainstream of human affairs. I relate more to an "individual," person-to-person level. I also am attracted to "counterculture" people, although not counterculture groups and the exclusiveness they sometimes foster. I think that individually, the CC types are more human, sensitive, and mellow. You're absolutely right about need for radical change, and any effort or movement to bring it about must involve all types of people—rich, poor, old, young, black, white, brown—all of the major segments of the society!! So, you see, I have a problem "fitting" into the group-oriented endeavor when the goals or aspirations of the group is narrow, exclusive, and elitist.

The psychological damage that prison does to the average sensitive person is truly awesome. It's like a raging beast that devours hope, respect, mind and selfness. It's a sort of mental brutality inflicted by the keepers, by unthinking "friends" that seem to forget about you when you're down. Neither men, women, children, nor animals were intended to be separated and caged.

Item: Men die violently in prison sometimes, as they do outside as well. But here life takes on such a cheapened aspect. They die for such trivial things! Things such as the offending of small sensitivities, a "cigarette" bet or debt, alienation of affection (contention and competition in prison "love affairs"). It really makes one aware of how terribly delicate the thread of life is . . . so at the mercy of blind arbitrary forces! It is so damn frightening! I can never become indifferent to any man's death. ". . . any man's death diminishes me . . ." John Donne, I believe. If there is an object lesson here it's this: Having seen men at their worst . . . and some at their best . . . I want to embrace life. I want to love it . . . nurture and protect it. I want to grab hold to "good" and never let go!

Make no mistake, prison is deadly! It's as many types of hell as there are types of prisoners here. And there are many, many types of prisoners here, every shape, size, color, temperament, or political affiliation. There are mass murderers, rapists, sex deviates, common thieves, sophisticated burglars and robbers, pimps, bums, aristocrats. And—this is important—there are men here so normal that their imprisonment is needless, and might justly be called a crime against humanity!

I have very high expectations for our friendship. I want to convey with all the power and insight I can, all the pain, agony, and small happinesses that makes up prisons. I want to establish a strong friendship bond that will penetrate these granite gray, tomb-like walls. I'd like our exchanging to be real, special, and mutually learning and fulfilling!

In the future I will tell you more about myself, the social/political/sexual dynamics of prison life, and lots more! Gotta close now until next time. Take care, brother, and please write soon.

Love, brotherhood
Charles

Dear Neil:

This is being written on Christmas Eve and probably won't reach you until after Christmas. How, and what, does a "long lost" brother say on the occasion of Christmas? It seems as if words, especially those spoken around Xmas, ring shallow and insincere. Anyway, however long we've been separated, or how far the physical distance is between us, I want you to know that I *do* think about you often and care for you. Nothing can, or will, ever change that! I hope you feel the same about me.

I haven't always been a brother you could be proud of, one that you'd necessarily want a closer association with, but I would hope that the new year will bring about renewed contact, understanding, and a much closer relationship. I read your comment in the G'ville *Sun* on Thanksgiving and I'm glad that you are happy about our renewed contact!

The end of another year is approaching, and the "end" is not in sight. I just hope to God that this will be the year they release me! The signs are encouraging. We have a new governor that's talking about reform, there is a renewed attack on the methods and procedures of parole, and there is a pretty strong effort underway to get rid of California's indeterminate sentence. I'll talk about the latter in another letter with you, OK? Then too, I've about got my requisite amount of time in as well. But that is precisely the problem: Under the "indeterminate sentence," you can only guess at what the requisite amount of time is. They have a sort of "blank check" on your life, and whether you are released or not can be as near or as close as whether a parole board member recovered from "too many" or whether he achieved sexual satisfaction the night before.

Ah well, I won't depress you any further with this dark mood of mine. I'd very much like to hear from you soon and wish you a Merry Christmas and Happy New Year. Take care and *please* write me when you get a chance, OK? Got to close. Peace and Love to you and your family!

Regards,
Charles

Dear Mrs. Wellman:

I'm sitting here on a Sunday morning and thought it would be a neat idea to drop you a short letter and a poem. Hope you got the last one.

I felt particularly moved to comment on something that surely all modern mothers are faced with—the exodus of their children from home. That seems terribly tragic . . . yet it's almost inevitable that they will leave to marry or establish their lives elsewhere! I was noting, with sorrow, that your kids are slowly moving out to start their lives. You know, George going to Hawaii, and Ellie talking about moving to Santa Barbara with Wendy and Steve. Ah, but enough sad reminiscing! So, how are you and your husband, are you well and in good health?

Christmas is always the time of year when I become depressed and downhearted. I guess it's because it's been so long, at least it seems that way, since I've known a Xmas of freedom! I really have to make an extra effort to avoid bringing up the emotions that goes through me during this period. But every letter, every thought expressed in those letters, gives me great comfort and joy because they tell me that someone cares . . . someone hasn't forgotten me. But I dare not pity myself, for self-pity would destroy the last shield I have against hopelessness and the bottomless pit of depression. Some day it's going to be over and I will walk out the gate a free man!

We've got a Poetry "Reading" today in the prison chapel. Guys who are involved in the Creative Writers Workshop and writer-poet guests from the outside will read their stuff. I'm really looking forward to it very much, looking forward to seeing and relating to the guests as much as hearing their poems and reading my own. We have so very little contact with "free people" here and there is a sort of temporary reconnecting process involved that's quite good for the morale. Letters help a lot in relieving some of the sense of isolation, but they can never replace the direct sensory experience of face-to-face talking and relating.

(I hope you will forgive this rambling, unorganized letter! I'm composing it at the typewriter and it is sort of a release valve . . . I just felt I had to talk to someone.)

I sure hope that I was able to answer some of your questions in the last letter! I got the feeling that I got carried away in it. I really wanted to give you a vivid word picture of what prison life is like. Too often, the written word seems so terribly inadequate for communicating the essence of an experience, know what I mean?

After the poetry reading: We were socked in by fog and they didn't release us until almost 12:00. So the meeting got off to a late start! Boy, was there a lot of energy and good vibes being given off!? The poetry was good, the people were really cool, sensitive, and understanding! All in all, a very nice trip!!

Well, I'll probably write you and Ellie again before Xmas, but if by chance I don't, I hope you'll both have a very nice Christmas! Oh, I'll make that definite, I *will* write again before Xmas, and I hope I'll get a letter from both of you, OK? Take care and write soon.

Love, Peace, Happiness
Charles

Dear Butch:

Sorry for not writing you sooner, man! There just ain't no good reason for not writing a friend, but as you can probably deduce, I've been feeling awfully shitty and "blown out," brother! Oh hell, I did write you a letter but it was (by my reckoning) pretty tepid and whining. Sorry 'bout that, but if I can't confide in you, a friend, who can I confide in . . . ?

Hey, I got *Belly Song* by Etheridge Knight from Broadside Press, also the *Berkeley Barb*. Thanx an awful lot!

Tell me something, huh? Why I'm so fond of you, Mimi, Pooh, and Bobo? Shit, I'm suppose to hate all honkies! Isn't that what the textbooks imply? That is, I'm suppose to be bitter, violent . . . an angry nigger frothing at the mouth.

Ah me, you been so fucking good to me . . . . . . I don't know if I'll ever be able to repay you for all the love and concern you've shown!! I say *fuck* the textbooks!! I'm not mad at my sisters and brothers, be they black/brown/white/yellow or chartreuse! I am mad at the *system*, this fucking system that has spawned so much evil and oppression, so many goddamn crooks and criminals masquerading as "leaders" and "upstanding" citizens!!

Seriously though, I've never hated *anything* too passionately, and that sorta scares me! I think that might be a plus for me . . . but I'm not so sure. Maybe I should at least have passed through a "hate" stage. You know, perhaps achieving some sort of catharsis or something!

Jesus, I've been thinking, I've really been a terrible correspondent the last month or so. You know, what few letters I did write were goddamn limp, flaccid, and insubstantial. Gotta watch that shit, man! I owe you a better accounting of myself and what the prison experience is about. I most certainly owe you a better literary output, in terms of sharing and exchanging our writings! I promise to do better in the future, brother.

Ah, but I know you'll understand though, when I say that there are days when I'm completely overwhelmed by the enormity of this awful shit here! Sometimes during these periods, it's almost as if my motor (read anyway you like) "shorts" out. It's these times when writing a letter becomes so hard. You know, you're striving not to be tepid, repetitious and inconsequential. You're trying to relate what's happening in a meaningful, dynamic way without an awful lot of bullshit rhetoric.

I think I've finally lifted myself from this deep dark depression now though. Thank God, I was beginning to think that my soul was *dead!*

Back to the need to hate something with a passion!: I hate the vague, abstract, "system," and the parasites that feed off the life of the people, but seems to me there should be something more . . . seems I should go to bed cussin' and wake up angry as hell.

Oh yeah, you wanted to hear or (see?) what the "solidarity handshake" has come to, right? Well, I can't graphically illustrate it for you as I'm not an artist, but I can try to explain it: Step #1, fingers and hand clasp in a "traditional" handshake; step #2, thumbs interlocked (this may be elaborated upon by covering the other party's entire hand with *your* left hand; step #3, fingers bent and interlocked with the hand of the other. There are dozens of variations of this and limited only by a person's imagination, but that is the "basic" solidarity shake.

Well, gotta close, man. I'll talk about violence in prison in the next letter, OK? Please write me soon OK? Hey, and remember, man, I LOVE you all—Mimi, Pooh, Bobo, everybody!! Keep your shit together and keep them cards and letters comin'!

LOVE
C

REHABILITATION

Billy Ray Johnson

I was taken away from society some three years ago; placed in custody and now live under a dictatorship here in prison. My attitude toward prison is dependent on how I'm treated by the officers who hold authority and who run this institution.

Prison is to me a family type of factory and I realize that I am locked down within it and within myself. This is a reality.

I strive for my freedom with my opposition, because the struggle is only mine to fight now and later on in life. My basic concern is getting the hell out of prison providing I keep my sanity and face up to being a mature man.

The only life I've ever known, prison society and things, don't change too much. A man has to create his own happenings just to stay aware of himself and remember the facts about being locked down inside prison. The danger that surrounds this oppressive environment is both depressing and unnecessary . . . but what can we do outside these facts? Talking too much is a risky business, difficult and very dangerous, because of the circumstance that could cause a man to lose his life. I've forced myself to play the psychological game but I watch what I say to other people . . . some prisoners are quick-tempered and most inmates don't think for themselves. In my opinion, most programs are set-up with those things in mind and are geared toward bringing the convict back to prison in a month, or a few years. The idea that rehabilitation is not working is not difficult to believe . . . it is a fact and everyone knows it. So we can't hide behind that.

I realized that I wanted to be free and that I was not motivated toward any purpose. As I instruct myself in that direction, I find myself feeling apart from this prison environment and no longer a product of it; I can think for myself because I know right from wrong and I realize what it is that I want out of life. All that I am doing is playing the hunches I get from myself. I like to think of myself as a humanitarian; but the interest is in myself, trying to reform my life instead of other people.

Books, like Dr. U. S. Andersen's *Three Magic Words* and Mr. W. C. Stone's *The Success System That Never Fails*, have helped me to change my attitude in the way in which I have it now and has been an aid in my thinking and mental attitude. That's how I instruct myself and how I remember the law which my mother gave me about God: I did not create myself and anyone who can change the world must be God. Any person who can change the world is God, but . . . not I.

In prison I try to think for myself and do for myself; I understand, there is not any type of program in prison in which a man can fully think for himself. However, I am obligated to design for myself a type of security program for the rest of my life. For the most part, prison is a warehouse for those men and women who don't think themselves worthy to live within society . . . and I am only trying to be fair to myself by giving myself a chance to live again, within the society I truthfully love. Be it as it must, my attitude is my feeling about myself, life and prison and I recognize the only thing changeable is myself.

My attitude toward prisons depends on how I'm treated by the officers who hold the authority positions in the institution. For one thing, I've learned from past experience that, if I let an officer affect my attitude, I'm telling him that I am not ready to be released from prison. So, I must at all cost, give attention to myself, stay on my job and keep myself under control with the realization that I am guiding my action and my personal growth, and the responsibility is all in my hands, to develop myself as more of a man than I was when I first came to prison.

I realize that there are officers who go out of their way to find a man trying to make something of himself and they try to get that man more time—if they can make him blow it . . . his mind. I believe that's part of their job—to test a man, to find out if he is ready for a release date and ready to move back into society.

My basic concern is getting the hell out of prison, fast . . . I want out and to be free in the highest sense of the word *freedom* (out of prison); not only environment, but freedom of mind as well as my spiritual soul. Freedom is the way I walk, the way I talk, the way I move around and the way I act. But to some degree, I am locked down within myself and inside this environment. I realize that's an attitude of mind, which is also a reality . . . and I am free at the same time. But, I strive for my freedom even in opposition to my struggle here in prison; I must make a better man of myself because there is more responsibility in my life.

A model is something used by an artist to serve as a pattern. Anyone can be an artist; we are responsible for our own imagination and create different patterns for ourselves. Society follows the rule of law because it's civilized and right. But society has ways of conditioning a person to think one way about what is right and what is wrong. Today there is a shortage of thinkers in our population who are creative enough to handle the situation with which we are faced. I realize that I am being modeled into a pattern that I have nothing to do with at all. But I try to build some type of life for myself from it. I've decided to write this part of life that I understand to be real only to myself . . . but it is real and it is life—the only life I've ever known. In just about every way you can imagine, I've spent some part of my life in a prison. I understand some of the conditions of prison but not all, none of what is happening in the handling of problems . . . but I'm learning about that also.

When I started doing prison time, just about everything was forced upon me. When to shave, when to eat, when to go to bed, when to have visitors, when to watch a movie, and where and when I was allowed to draw my money from the canteen and how much.

The model of society is conformity to the rules of law. The social restrictions placed upon the individual are a model within a model. Therefore, he or she must conform to the law and common guidelines set toward obedience within society. The model within affects individual freedom, and sets a mood toward conformation to the greater model. By the same token, prisoners in the State of California's Department of Corrections are faced with the same type of unrest and uneasiness because of the guidelines and restrictions.

Living in prison as I am today under a dictatorship isn't my idea of good leadership. Especially when my writing is censored and often times causes me to conceal my expression of prison life and keep my emotions down to a minimum. Maybe the national population has no idea what it means for a person to live under a dictatorship and the person who has never been to prison would find my story difficult to believe. I can understand it because I know what it is like, what the majority of the population is living under—a democratic government. And one day I will return to society a changed man, having undergone a different type of mental change than most free citizens living within society today.

I realize that I am being modeled in one way or another and, at best, I try not to worry about it. Providing I keep my sanity and my mind on constructive things which have to do with my own plans of rehabilitating myself. That's the hidden model I'm building for myself. In my personal opinion, the Department of Corrections does very little toward rehabilitating a prisoner.

During the three years since I was taken from society, placed in custody as a prisoner, now living under a dictatorship, I have had no rights that are my very own . . . not even free expression. Just about everything is limited or restricted to and for prisoners. For example, I am not allowed to use the telephone for any reason without authorized permission. And if I do, I am to give my name and prison number to the person at the other end and explain the reason for calling that number. I am permitted to have little in the way of personal property. I am permitted to write ten people at any time and I am expected to consider that a privilege and not a right. I have the *privilege* of visiting with ten approved visitors but not at the same time. They, my visitors, are expected to visit me only within the approved restricted area.

I realize the danger that surrounds this oppressive environment. The danger is in the institution authorities lurking in the dark and waiting for a mistake to happen so they can take full advantage of the situation . . . in one way or the other. Living in prison is a risky business because there are many circumstances that can cause a man to lose his life. Maybe over a punk, or a box of cigarettes. So a man has to be aware of the situation in his environment at all times.

In my 12 x 4 cell, I have many fears. One of them is losing my personal identity to this administration. That's why I am working toward my own rehabilitation in hope that I can keep what's mine.

The gray walls of prison are no joke and doing this time is for real. I am called a thing and sometimes when I am needed for some type of work I am called by name, or more usually by prison number. I realize I am treated as less than a man and there isn't much I can do about it except accept it as part of my reality for right now. But the whole idea behind rehabilitation is to learn how to accept one's own reality, whether in prison or out there in society.

A man in prison often carries himself much differently than what he would carry himself out there in society. In prison it's understood that one will have to accept much hardship from the environment and the officials, not to mention the other inmates.

If I should lose control over my attitude while in prison, I set my own time back a few years because a convict is expected to keep himself together and refrain from hostile attitudes. Prison is a place of correction and the man should know better and think before he acts. It's just that simple . . . if he wants out of prison.

The entire show is the playing of a psychological game with the mind, which is a part of the punishment of doing prison time. I've forced myself to play the game and accept this part of reality as being vitally necessary to my personal growth now and later on in society. But at this moment my thinking is geared toward understanding myself and this disgusting condition I wake up to every morning. I watch what I say to other people because there are so many men wanting to go back to the society that they (inmates) would do anything and tell anything in hopes of getting an early date from the Adult Authority Board of Release. But not only that, some prisoners are quick-tempered and it's best to remember that they are a part of your reality.

As everyone in here realizes, they are faced with the indeterminant sentence. It's understood generally that convicts try and respect one another by staying out of each other's way—in some prisons that's not always understood. Most men in prison today are not thinking for themselves, partly because of the different programs set up within different institutions. The process of taking orders from a servant of society keeps most men (prisoners) separate from their own personal thinking and making the necessary decision of what's right and wrong for themselves. In my opinion, there is very little understanding given willingly to the convict.

Rehabilitating a prisoner to take orders is not rehabilitating toward responsibility and respect for the law. Very little is being done to upgrade the prisoner's level of thinking and skills . . . it's an attitude of "I just don't care."

In my opinion, few inmates understand the importance of the educational program set-up in prison for their own benefit. That, too, I am using to rehabilitate myself and try to promote a better understanding of myself. Those who understand the educational system are utilizing it right now to their personal benefits.

As far as I am concerned, I'm locked up in prison behind stone walls, concrete and iron and steel, but I have hopes of being released from custody one day and returned to society a changed man.

PRISON DAYS

John D. Johnston

Despite the fairy tales about prison being a place for rehabilitation there exists here nothing that remotely resembles
a therapeutic environment. In residence is one overworked
psychiatrist who doesn't have the required independence
from the prison system to perform the complex task of
assisting inmates with psychological problems or help
people having sociopathic personalities deal with the outside world. For the most part group counseling is headed
by uniformed guards motivated more by the additional
paycheck to handle inflated mortgages rather than profes-
sional dedication. Here also in abundance are guns, guns
for blowing a man's brains out to erase all his mental problems with astounding suddenness and acute finality.

With this psychosis-inducing atmosphere intensified
by the added pressure of undefined time, how does the
prisoner maintain his frail sanity? Each of us approach the
problem differently, many fail and go crazy. Those who
go crazy meet one of two fates: they are either relegated to
the walking dead with drugs furnished by large commer-

cial legitimatized dope pushers, or those particularly acute are reduced to bleeding lumps of flesh with the bite from 30 caliber killing machines.

I wish to remain sane and alive so I let the accumulated anger and frustration engendered by the absurdity of prison's illogical logic dissipate in words. In order to help preserve a balanced mind I laugh a lot and keep a diary. I find the diary to be very quieting stilling my restless psyche. The following are two day's entries.

Monday, October 28

Morning: Today is the day that Debbie comes, all my actions center around her visit.
That Night: I got up early this morning and went through my hygiene routine, gargled, brushed my teeth, washed my face over the little sink, splashed water everywhere, wetting everything. Because showers are staggered, we did not shower last night so I packed my little sack with underwear, socks and a towel to shower out on the yard.

When I got outside the weather was cold and cloudy so I postponed the cold shower hoping the day would warm up.

I walked around to the recreation area, stood and watched the water from the early morning's rain drain off the baseball diamond. The swirling water had practically hypnotized me when Tippy came up. He and I have running discussions on varying topics. Today we got into the purpose of human beings and if a purpose existed what was it. We also talked about the drive, some of us experience, to read, trying to gather knowledge about anything that could be used towards survival. We talked about the force pushing us to find a higher purpose and order to all this chaos.

The discussion continued for two hours, until 10 o'clock. Cold, I decided to go in on the 10 o'clock line. On the way in I met C. B. coming out to braid my hair on the yard. We returned to the cold yard, he braided me up in time to make the chow line.

For lunch we had soup and a pretty good tuna salad. Like all good foods, however, we were only allowed one scoop. Little Al sat at the table with us and told C. B. he was being called for a visit. Little Al was also expecting a visit but it was overdue and he was getting a little nervous.

After lunch it's mandatory that we go to the yard, so out we went. I shot a few baskets in between cutting it up with Jimmy about the expected visit. The sun came out so I figured on trying the shower again.

I walked around to the shower area, undressed, laid my stuff out, twisted the knob and waited, nothing. The water hadn't been turned on for the day. It was almost 12:30. I didn't figure I had time to find the guard to turn the water on before the 12:30 line, so I dressed, packed my stuff up and split.

Saw my homeboy Joe, cutting it up with Ted about the subways, the traffic and New York City in general so I joined them for a while. The P.A. system called 12:30 line going in and I went in with it.

When I got in my cell I took a sink bath. Little Al came by still anxiously anticipating his unarrived visit; so was I, but there was no point in both of us verbalizing it. Suddenly all manner of water started coming out of the sky in great big body drenching drops. They called rainy day lockup. Everyone was soaked before they could cross the yard.

The runner came to my cell to let me know I had a visit. Hurrying now, I finished putting my clothes on, attitude changing instantly knowing I would be out there with that woman.

When the guard pulled the bar for the people coming in I was gone; down the tier, down three flights of iron steps, out through the first steel door, waited a few minutes for the guard to take his time to open the outside gate, then out into the yard. I crossed the yard dodging puddles as I go to keep my visiting shoes from getting messed up, the rain had stopped, in to five-count gate, telling the bull I got a visit, through five building, down the hallway, past the kitchen, up the stairs to two building, turn right, past some people taking showers, hollered at Penny as I went by his cell.

I get to the visiting room door and bang on it until the light over the intercom comes on. I holler my name and number, "Johnston B-25589," so they can check the book and push the button to let me in. When the buzzer releases the door, I pull it open, step inside and shut it behind me, walk down some stairs and stand in front of a wire mesh door until the guard opens it with his key. I step in and to the right into a little room where the visitors can't see the guard feeling all over my body while he checks for the need of a haircut, shave or any non-regulation appearance; then out into the visiting room full of light and sweet women smells.

I have to go over to the big court-bench-looking desk to register in, the woman guard working there politely says, "hello," and tells me where my seat is.

Just as I sat down Debbie came in. Alive and smiling she walks around the crowded visiting room. We met, hugged and kissed and hugged some more, using one of our two hugs and kisses but stretching them out as long as practical, trying to feel each other as close as possible.

We sat down on the opposite sides of the table as required, talked about any and everything trying to rush to get things said in the available time. Not being able to stay so far apart we take a chance and move the table out of the way, hold hands, touch and feel each other's warmth.

During the visit we got up a few times to take some pictures and get something to drink, always clinging tight to each other. We came back to our seats, touch and stare suggestively at each other. Every once in awhile we break the spell, look at C.B., make faces and laugh. Not too much time is spent doing this, time in the visiting room is precious.

3 o'clock comes too quickly, they call visiting over for the day. This is the hated part of the visit, separation. We use up our other alloted hug and kiss. Oblivious to the crowd around us we made this more extended, intense, arousing, energizing and draining at the same time. At the door we sneak another quick kiss, then she is gone.

I stood around awkwardly for a few minutes trying to get myself together and come down. The sergeant called for the people in one building and I prepared to get shook down.

In the shakedown room I had to take off each piece of clothing so the guard can look through them. First my clothes, my shirt, pants, shoes, socks and underwear, then me, in my mouth, under my nuts as I shake my penis at him, I turned spread, he looks in my ass, under each foot. I get dressed.

The trip back to my cell is like an obstacle course with gates, hallways, doors, locks, latches, bolts and bars, but I am filled with energy and the presence of that healthy young woman, so I make it.

Back in my cell I don't turn on the light, but sit in the semi-darkness contemplating her existence filled with love and energy, all the things lacking in here. It will be a long wait until next Monday, besides that is another day and the future is not promised us. At least today was done smooth and easy in the warm laughter of a woman.

Friday, November 1

Just after breakfast the whistle blew, a chilling sound cutting right to my bones. In response, the gunrail bull went running down the gunrail past our cell, gun in ready position, keys, flashlight and other junk rattling as he went by. The buzzer also went off summoning the emergency crew of guards. There is a guy standing on our tier narrating. He can see the guards running up the stairs and he says someone just got "arrested."

I looked out the window in front of my cell and I saw that there were six guards escorting a black prisoner across the yard to the captain's office. A white prisoner was being escorted to the five-building count gate by two guards. (I wonder why it only took two guards for the white and six for the black.)

I hoped like hell it was only a fist fight and headup. Anything else involving blacks and whites could unleash a holocaust.

On the 8 o'clock line I went out to see what had happened. On the yard I got the scam. A white prisoner threw some shit on a black and the black instantly got off, in his ass. There appeared to be no motivation for the shit slinging, the white is known to be nuts. Anyhow, the guard got to the scene late and only saw the black dude beating the other dude's ass so he threatened to shoot who he thought was the aggressor. Some other black prisoners watching the whole thing started hollering at the gunrail bull not to shoot and threatened him with curses and screams. He didn't shoot but only blew his whistle.

That incident could have easily been something else. A person could have lost his life because of an unprovoked attack or a too quick trigger finger. That black could have been me if I had happened to be walking by when that nut had the urge to throw his shit. A few different circumstances and my life would have been in jeopardy.

At 10 o'clock I came back in. I was not in my cell but a few minutes when I heard the penetrating sound of the whistle blowing again. I can tell from the sound that it is on the yard so I rush to my bars to see if I can spot what happened. Six guards are running with a stokes stretcher and a person is hanging loosely in it. By the rushing I can tell the person is hurt bad. After a while I saw another group of guards escorting someone across the yard. Then they came back and took half the people in the domino area away. Two incidents of violence and it is not yet 12 o'clock.

For a while the cell block was real quiet. Quietness, just like life here, is tenuous. In the respite from noise I began to think about how I struggle to get out while people on the street, not able to conceive of the nearness of chaos and death, ask me to wait. They easily dismiss my request for help by saying it will come sometime, just be patient. I cannot be patient and I cannot idly wait on others to decide whether my life or my existence is worth their immediate involvement. The dictates of survival demand that I do anything and practically everything to survive and get out of this trap. I can indulge in idealistic dreams after I get out but until then . . .

After the whistle following the last incident, the gunrail bull came running around to see what had happened. He asked was there a man down and was it a convict. Someone on the tier above me hollered it was a human being. I doubt he got the significance of that comment because he, like all his fellow guards, are programmed to see a difference in the hurt, suffering and death of prisoners. How else could they so easily carry guns to shoot us with?

It is a cold, grayish cloudy day. Everyone walking the yard is wrapped up extra tight with collars turned up and hats pulled down. A sad, gray Folsom day. Death hangs in the air like a thick woolen blanket. Someone must be claimed before it will pass. Everyone waits apprehensively hoping it won't come or if it does it will claim another.

I pose a question to myself: who is it that gives us life? Not an easy question and one philosophers, theologians and scientists have been trying to answer for years. Just like all weighty questions this one engenders others. Do our parents give us life? Is it the mailman who brings the birthday gift the giver? No. Are our parents then the givers of life or just the deliverers? I do not know.

Well, a guy just brought me the scam, Bad News was

the one who got stabbed and he died. Bad News, a guy who was on death row but because of the change in law escaped being executed. Knowing his case I knew that he had a good change of getting out and his chances were increasing. Things were falling into place, a real lucky guy, now he's gone. I guess his luck ran out.

He was on our basketball team, he was my "client," in fact, he was also my friend. Folsom has claimed him. This makes the second person I knew closely to die within a couple of weeks. California prisons are death-oriented, a true waste of humanity.

Under different conditions, Bad News would be alive, but this not-so-great society forces us into useless but unpreventable internecine battles and death situations. Until we change the conditions and attack with full force the source of the plan, scheme and design of genocide, we will continue to eat each other alive.

The sun is coming out, death must be satisfied for today.

OH LONELY NIGHT

Kel

I think and act as an individual. My thoughts are my own, but, if the real truth were revealed, you could say they reflect the thoughts of the majority of prisoners behind bars.

We have two personalities. One that we show to our associates and the one we keep hidden and only bring out in the dark of night.

The first, the hard-nosed convict, not giving a damn whether tomorrow comes or not. Laughing at the efforts of rehabilitation, cursing the officials and damning society in general. We change our camouflage like chameleons, from one group to another. Becoming a radical when with a radical group and showing our intellect when with intellectuals. We create problems for ourselves to give a reason for our existence. Gambling for picayune stakes that become large because of the value we place on them, playing mental games with each other, and never, never letting the opponent know when he has touched a soft spot. We do anything to forget the three hundred and sixty-five days that has just been handed us by a stroke of the pen.

Another denial, so what? But underneath is a boiling, seething cauldron ready to scald any who might chance to pierce that thick veneer.

We learn to recognize the warning signals of each individual and pull back quickly when they are flashed. Life is very cheap unless it is your own that is in jeopardy. There are many ways to release the built-up tension, if you have the talent. Myself, I choose the physical exertion of basketball, but even then there are heated arguments that can turn into a life-or-death situation if the proper finesse is not used.

We have to learn to adapt quickly to any situation. Those who don't are eliminated or used by the strong. It is a constant battle of wits and strength.

There is no time for thoughts of your loved ones, no time to plan for the future. This is your future! This is the daytime convict you see walking the yard, the one with a mask so thick it couldn't be cracked with a sledgehammer.

There is a certain time of the day that eyes begin turning towards the clocks hanging in view. A restlessness is felt and lines begin to form. It is nearing three o'clock.

It is time to readjust the mind, time to relax the stern rigidity of the yard convict. An anxiety begins to build for the letter that might be waiting . . . mail call is only an hour away.

The cell blocks gobble up the long lines of men and soon the yard is empty with the exception of feeding birds and a few stray cats. Each man waits in front of his assigned cell. Some are more fortunate than others and have no cellmate. The majority are doubled up. Two men living in a four-by-ten cubicle can and do create space problems, but, we adjust to that too. With the exception of supper, we will be locked in this small space together for the next seventeen hours. A car thief might be paired with the most hardened of criminals.

There are thirty-one cells to a tier and there are five tiers, there are four sections to a block, A, B, C, D and on each bunk in each cell there is a man waiting for word from outside. I lie on my bunk, eyes closed, listening for a certain sound. The scuff, scuff of brown polished shoes accompanied by the jingle of keys . . . I await with bated breath, and, as he pauses to call out a name, my heart races with the adrenalin of false hope. Then, the cold, sinking pain as he passes without a glance. That lonely, hurt thing within me scrambles after the disappearing brown-clad back with a hope that he has made a mistake. Dejectedly, it returns to wait for another tomorrow, another mail call.

The immediate feeling is to strike out at anyone or anything to cover up that forgotten, hurt, little self within me. It is a mental battle that is fought over and over. Sometimes the battle is lost by those who haven't learned to control *the Mask*, and invariably there is a fight that could end drastically if not smoothed over by a sincere apology.

After a drab, flavorless meal, we return to our cells and settle down to the routine of many nights that have passed and the many that are still to come. It is a time to write letters or to work on a cell hobby. Painting, leather working, woodcraft or knitting. I have my own type of escape. I am a poet at heart and I let my emotions out through my poetry. I find that I can create a character and move him about through the plot of a story or a poem. I enjoy the freedom of saying what I feel, but there is a limit of time, even in the cells. There is a period that all noises must cease and this means my typewriter as well as the hammering of leather tools or musical instruments. It is nine-thirty P.M. a hush falls over the building like a blanket. Last minute preparations are being made before the lights are turned out. I crawl into my bed knowing that sleep is still far off. This is the time for that other personality to emerge.

Lying there with my face turned to the wall, I am fully aware of the total aloneness. It is a feeling of utter futility, a helplessness, and I clench my fists trying to stave off the flood of fantasies that are hovering there at the edge of my consciousness. It is no use. Pictures of my wife and children are imposed on my brain. A stifled sob escapes from deep within for the letter that did not come. I conjur up scenes from the past. Scenes that are painful to remember but impossible to hold off. My emotions run the gamut of hate, anger, self-pity, thoughts of revenge, all of them are a cover for the hidden guilt that I feel, but I love, even though my wife is living with another man, I still love and it is a cause for thoughts that flash through my brain like strobe lights, a cause for the frustration of knowing I can do nothing about it, so I create a world of fantasy of how I would like it to be, but always on the edge pushing its way in, is the reality of how it is. I cry like a child for I am deeply hurt, I cry silently, inside. There is my sister whom I have not seen for twenty years and I try to channel my thoughts in that direction but I always return to a dream that can never be again. I wonder when it will end, if ever. How long will I go on torturing myself with such thoughts, and each night it is the same thing over and over again? Insanity always seems to be around the next tomorrow.

I never know when sleep comes. It is a sheer exhaustion on the body and mind. When it can take no more, my eyes close and a numbness overcomes me.

When I awaken, it is with a reluctance for I know that soon I will have to face another day like yesterday and all the yesterdays that have gone before. I adjust the daytime mask that has slipped during the night and prepare myself for the battle of wits and games that are soon to begin. I try not to think of the night that is coming. A night of fear, fantasy and pain, another night of futile frustration, a dreaded night, a silent night, oh lonely, lonely night. . . .

DAILY NOTES FROM A HIDING PLACE

Lanners L. X.

Prison life is perpetual stress, an ordeal of unreal reality. These notes are the results of thoughts and afterthoughts, incidents and encounters with the prison condition as it occurs within me. I have risen from good and bad dreams, even nightmares, and recorded them to read back over later to see if I have crossed the line that divides sanity from insanity. Tomb dwelling can become habit forming . . . .

9/14

Because self-preservation is the first law of nature, knowledge of this law is 90 percent of success. But being successful means different things to different people. It is these differences that cause man to deviate from natural law, leaving him to toil under superimposed man-made laws that say: "Ignorance of the law is no excuse."

As I trip over all the unfulfilled years I've wasted away in this tomb of living dead, my despair sinks to rock bottom with the image of my children, who asked the last

65

time they saw me, "When are you coming home, daddy?"
Their voices now register in the bass and baritone range,
instead of the light tinkle I remember from their childhood.
And I tell my mirrored image that the scalp I see shining
through my rapidly thining hair is simply the result of ner-
vousness—not declining age. In a futile effort to escape
these painful thoughts I turn on the TV and begin to watch
"law & order" dance across the screen. But the keeper of
the keys comes along even to spoil that trip: "Your TV's
too loud, either put your earphones on or turn it off!"

"They're broke," I reply wanly.

"Well, get them fixed!"

"I don't have any money to get them fixed."

"Well, that's not my problem, so you'll have to give
up the TV or turn it off!"

The same forces outside that makes a man violate the
law exist in here as well. The criminal is still allowed to
prey on the poor, and because I have no money I must be
victimized, forced in a corner, forced to survive.

It's coat pullin' time/
where mind scenes are questioned and overkill is ever
present.
Flashbacks of overcrowded canteen lines extorting
and fleecing/
hot relentless sun on bared heads/
and rerun TV programs for the second time sucks up
energy.
There are prison school teachers who dare to ask that
we bare our souls to the hot suns of controlled
society. After years of being in a position of this
nature one cannot expect a man to be a free spirit.

9/15

I am bombarded by millions of suggestions, both audio
and video. At times I detect other forces that demand a
test. Impositions by impostors make it almost impossible
to do one's own thing—whatever that is! I lie on my bunk
and listen to the crackle of souls in the night, souls that

neither toil nor spin, souls of con/victims of a thing machine. Thing machines don't honor human life, let alone their dreams. Thing machines only protect property, the property of evildoers, the criminals of the universe. They claim all the booty copped in the many capers pulled right under our noses, before our very eyes, from within our beings.

9/16

The mornings are so quiet and peaceful, making this tomb that much more macabre. I think about my children and the years I have been deprived of them—and they of me.

I guess I'll stay in all day because I just want to think and introspect. Things are changing so fast that it's a job to keep up with them all. I wonder what my children are doing? Do they ever think of me, and how?

This amazing madness we call life is really a test. It's so full of traps and pitfalls, with all sorts of filthy birds just waiting to take advantage of other's misfortunes. The blues ain't nothing but unfinished episodes that long for completion.

9/17

Like dreams broken into by mind robbers, it's count time again. Stand up to the bars so they can see if you're still enduring a corpse's existence. Then the bull delivering the mail passes my cell without even a glance in my direction. Wait! He's coming back. I'm crushed with disappointment again, as it's nothing but a chrono from the Screening Committee notifying, as per usual, that my request for a reduction in custody has been denied.

> Endless demands made on my life/
> as if I'm not to expect anything of it/
> but changes . . .
> Hey!
> I be sounding like/
> paranoid bleeding hearts/
> looking for ways out of sick bodies.

9/18

Another morning, a different-yet-same thing in the tomb. Today is already yesterday and tomorrow at once. As usual my mind is on my freedom.

Mzaha, my beautiful Brother of the tomb, the house of the devil. Your soul is free but your body is locked and boxed in. Yet you continue to resist, to struggle—so involved 'til time seems to lose its scent. The stench of death speaks louder than anything I've ever heard. It goes straight to the brain—a smell so foul, so overpoweringly foul that after it assails your senses it leaves you with no doubt of its absolute message of finality. Finality! Finality! Finality!

9/19

I lay quietly in the cold chilly night, alone and lonely, thinking of all I miss so much, as the soft morning approaches peacefully—chasing the darkness away. O for the warmth of my bed, when it's shared with . . . . The sudden shock of reality when Zenzell comes and snuggles up between us. I play possum and she kisses my eyes, nose and mouth, and then sits back to watch my reactions, with big bright, brown eyes filled with delight and anticipation.

> Rigid frigidity of the mind/
> is certainly a cause for alarm/
> so from the gates of insanity/
> I broomed.
> Leaving behind/
> the bizarre/
> the wicked and tempting death . . .

ANOTHER NIGHT OF FRUSTRATION

Ross Laursen

The cell reeks with frustration again tonight. The two ten-foot long rectangular walls, old greeting cards neatly pasted up on the one side and huge Swissair calendar photographs stuck up on the other, squeeze coldly in on me and mock my very human existence. I force my aging, aching body to stand boldly in the center of this concrete coffin, my arms outstretched, my hands pressing agonizingly against the walls, and a voiceless scream explodes from the belly of my brain, "I'm not guilty, you sonofabitches! In my veins is the blood of Comanche warriors! In my veins is the blood of Viking chieftans! I refuse to betray my heritage! I'll not say I'm guilty and take you bastards and your foul-smelling, criminal justice system off the hook! You KNOW I'm not guilty! Damn you! Damn you!"

Resting between my feet on the worn concrete floor is a small piece of white paper that reads: Laursen, Ross. B-26430. Executive Meeting 11-12-74 of Adult Authority, Sacramento. Application for parole: DENIED.

Nine years and five months of clean institutional record. WORTHLESS! An earned high school diploma. WORTHLESS! An earned diploma from the Central Bible College of Springfield, Missouri. WORTHLESS! Three awards earned from the School of Journalism of the Southern Illinois University at Carbondale for outstanding reportage on the prison newspaper. WORTHLESS! Seven certificates of completion earned from the Salvation Army Bible Study Division. WORTHLESS! Nine terms as Chairman of the Creative Writers' Workshop. WORTHLESS! Print Shop Clerk two years. WORTHLESS! Cannery Clerk two years. WORTHLESS! Protestant Chaplain's Clerk four years. All WORTHLESS!

My impulse is to reach down, scoop up the freedom-denying paper, wad it into a ball in my fist and throw it through the sickly green bars at the front of the cell. But I don't. I've learned over the years that I must keep every scrap of these life-stealing bits of paper as court exhibits at my never-ending legal war with the Adult Authority. Otherwise, without them, I make it too damn easy for the prosecution prone courts to deny me also!

I gingerly put the official results of the Adult Authority away in a large, green, three-ring folder marked "Exhibits" and take down another binder marked "Affidavits." There it is! Something that no other imprisoned accused kidnapper in the world has. A signed notarized affidavit by the "victim" Donald Mark Teeter stating plainly: "Laursen is *not* the man who kidnapped me on October 14, 1964 in Fresno, California. Laursen was wrongly convicted. He is innocent."

Damn the Adult Authority! For three years they've been in possession of Teeter's sworn affidavit absolving me of his kidnapping. Each year one of their members dramatically reads it aloud in the hushed board room while I sit there on my chair in the center of the room foolishly praying that this year it'll be different. But it's the same. Every year it's the same.

"The jury found you guilty, Laursen, so we've got to assume you're guilty." Always delivered with that we're-the-Pharisees-who-crucified-Christ smile! "We're going to submit you for a full en banc hearing of the board. You've been made a Special Case. Since you won't admit your guilt we can't promise you anything . . . you understand that?"

Understand it? My hands shake as I think about it. Understand that there is no such thing as JUSTICE in the world? That the Constitution of the United States is a bad joke? That men have never—in the long memory of recorded history— had compassion one for another?

Every year it's always the same. "No, Sir. I don't understand that. I'm not guilty! I never kidnapped Donald Mark Teeter. Mr. Teeter freely admits that I'm not the man who kidnapped him. You people in 1970 paroled the kidnapper. Vincent Roosevelt Lowrie. You have his affidavit there. He admits under oath that he's the kidnapper. He also admits under oath that I wasn't his accomplice. Mr. Teeter swears that Lowrie was his kidnapper and that I wasn't Lowrie's accomplice. They both KNOW that I'm not guilty."

"Well, the jury found you guilty, Laursen. We have to go by their verdict." Year after year the cop-out answer never varies. I go before different board members each year but the cop-out answer is always the same: "The jury found you guilty."

Before putting the "Affidavit" binder back on the law-book-filled wooden shelf I pause long enough to read again— for the millionth time—the sworn affidavit of eye-witness Theresa Holtzman. "I witnessed the kidnapping of Donald Mark Teeter in Fresno, California, on October 14, 1964. Ross Laursen is *not* the man I saw assisting Lowrie kidnap Teeter on that date."

The words never change. Only the pages on the Salvation Army calendar hung up over the too-clean sink change. Slowly I pass my large rough hand over my face. I was 35 years old when arrested. I'm going on 46 now. And tonight the too small cell that has become my living tomb is reeking with frustration again.

EPILOGUE

I was born on a hot Friday August afternoon in the little silver mining town high up in the Rocky Mountains of Colorado, named after the famed Indian, Chief Ouray.

My grandfather, a rough, rawboned Viking from Denmark, was the sheriff of the county and his greatest headache was my brawling, hard drinking, hardworking Dad, who everybody mistakenly called "Swede." The brawling youngster once went nine rounds in Durango with tough and clever Rocky Mountain Heavyweight Champion Sid Belt before being decked and counted out. Years later I squared things for "Swede" by KOing Sid's son Bob Belt in the second round of the main event at the Legion Hall in Cortez—turned out, unlike his old man, the "Kid" was a sucker for a good left hook.

Jackie, my mother, was a beautiful raven-haired, hazel-eyed, fiery Comanche-English woman who, on a cloudy day in an alley behind our house in Montrose, Colorado, pumped five .38 slugs into "Swede's" brain. They buried "Swede" high up on a mountain side, next to one of his two silver mines, overlooking the city of Ouray. The raven-haired, hazel-eyed beauty, was brought to trial by a jury of her "peers" and found guilty of manslaughter. She was shipped off to prison in Cañon City and her son Ross and daughter Rosalie were unceremoniously bundled off to St. Mary's Orphanage in Pueblo.

After Jackie had pulled her "bit" in Cañon City she came to Pueblo and got my sister and I and we went to live in Aspen, Colorado, where she met and married a big hulk of a man named "Slim" Marshall. With a lot of hard work and little capital, Jackie and "Slim" built and operated the

Silver Dollar Bar & Grill—the finest cafe and miners' bar in the town. One summer's night, after a heated quarrel, Jackie dissolved the partnership with "Slim" by chasing him down the alley with a meat cleaver in her hand. Seems Jackie had a "thing" about "holding court" in alleys. Two months later, on Halloween night, "Slim" got even with Jackie by setting fire to the back of the grill and bar and in the process managed to burn down a beauty parlor, a hotel, Huey the Blindman's candy store, Old Man Tate's Pool Hall, Mike's Ski Shop, and a drugstore that was next to the grill. "Slim" was a volunteer fireman and although it was common knowledge that he'd set the fire it could never be proven in a court of law.

After the fire the three of us, Jackie, myself and my sister Rosalie, moved to Cortez, Colorado. Charlie's Drive Inn in Cortez was a large restaurant-garage-3.2-beer-bar-dance-hall-honky-tonk where five people had gone bankrupt because of the rowdy Four Corners crowd that hung out there and did bloody battle every Friday and Saturday night in the parking lot.

The man who owned the place was a local politician who also ran the city gas company and was a good friend and financial backer of the local sheriff. The two of them, the politician and the sheriff, offered Charlie's Drive Inn to Jackie, with carte blanc to do whatever was necessary to straighten the joint out and make it a paying business. Well, after Jackie shot three would-be-tough guys and messed up one dude's face with a broken Coor's bottle, the place got to be so orderly and quiet it was renamed Jackie's Drive Inn and the Kiwanis and Rotary Clubs held their monthly dinners there.

Horace Holt was a pencil-mustached ladies' man who owned one of the three barbershops in Cortez and was greatly admired locally for being the best deer hunter and draw-poker player in town. When he and Jackie got married, over the strenuous objections of her twelve-year-old son—me!—a deal was made with Father Edward J.

Flanigan to accept the "objectionable boy" as a so-called "citizen" of Boys Town located just outside Omaha, Nebraska on a high, cold and windy hill—in consideration, of course, of a "donation" amounting to $125 paid each month to the Good Father.

At Boys Town I soon learned that the oldest and toughest kid there was the "elected" Mayor and his cronies made up the ten governing council members officiously called "Commissioners." I was rudely awakened before dawn every morning by the bleating of a half-frozen-lipped kid trying to be Ziggy Ellman on an old beat-up trumpet, then stood in line for an hour in front of the Mess Hall while one of the "Commissioners" tried to determine which dormitory line looked the straightest and got to go in first; then sat at a six-man table and took my "blue john" and oatmeal *after* the "Table Captain" sat down, raked off what little cream there might be on top of the pitcher of blue john for himself, and had his fill of the oatmeal.

After breakfast I had to straighten up beds and buff the tile floor in my dormitory wing. Then it was school till lunch, then back to school, then wash all the windows on one floor of the school building before supper, then back to school for an hour study period, and finally to bed and lights out to "taps" played by the same bad-lipped kid.

Because I refused to attend Mass and wouldn't write glowing letters of "how nice it is here" to Jackie, I was "promoted" to the Boys Town Sick Boys Club where I had the special privilege every Saturday, aside from my other chores, of cleaning up the Mayor-Commissioners' dormitory, then spending the rest of the afternoon dogtrotting around the dormitory quadrangle.

I put up with this total madness for nearly a year. Then, one exceptionally cold December night, I and another "dissatisfied boy" hoofed it out of there and hitchhiked our way to Denver, where my adopted aunt Billie Snapp fed us before calling Jackie, who immediately called the Denver police, who arrested us and tossed us into the infamous 9th & Pearl detention home.

Father Flanigan, although world renowned for his oft repeated statement that "there is no such thing as a bad boy," took the other kid back but refused to accept me— giving for his reasons that I was the "ring-leader" of the two. Aunt Billie talked Old Man Byers of the prestigious private Byers Home For School Boys in Denver into accepting me at a healthy $300 a month fee.

Two years later I had an unfortunate dispute with Old Man Byers about being forced to attend his summer camp again and went A.W.O.L. to Cortez where Jackie and Horace let me work around the Drive Inn long enough to buy a sleeping bag and save up $8. Then I hit the highway for California. Jackie and Horace were later divorced, remarried for the second time, divorced again, and later Horace killed Grace Lattimore with one of his prized deer rifles in the Green Frog Saloon in Natirita, Colorado, then managed to cut his own throat with his straight razor and died in Montrose General Hospital, like "Swede."

Ruby and Myron MacPeck were two very special and wonderful people who were engaged in building the 500-unit China Lake Trailer Park in Ridgecrest, California, for the use of construction workers building the Naval (Ordinance) Test Station there. They took me in, gave me a job, paid me a monthly wage, and sent me to school over at Trona.

One summer, when I was fifteen years old, a robust six feet tall, and tipping the scales at a hard 190 pounds (I weigh over 300 and stand 6'2" today!), I went down to Draft Board #41 in Bakersfield and lied about my age so that I could get a summer job with the Navy at the Test Station. Two months later I was drafted. Seems there was a war going on and they could use guys like me! Two years later, when World War II was ended, I was honorably discharged at Fort Douglas, Utah, after spending nearly nine months in an Army hospital at Camp Bowie, Texas.

With an Honorable Discharge in my pocket I went to Las Vegas, Nevada, and started stacking chips on a roulette table in the old Frontier Club downtown, where the Golden Nugget stands now. I worked the night shift and attended Clark County High School four hours every afternoon. By the time I was nineteen, I was running a low-ball game of my own in the Glenn Rondezvous Club in Newport, Kentucky, where I shot a man in an argument over a sizeable pot—this got me a three-year term in the state reformatory at LaGrange.

I was twenty-one years old when the police in Louisville, Kentucky, mistakenly arrested me for allegedly being the leader of a gang of stick-up men who, among other things, were charged with robbing the Inman Furniture Company of its payroll.

Armed robbery in the Commonwealth of Kentucky at that time called for a sentence of life imprisonment or death. I was tried for the electric chair and the jury, behind the testimony of only one alleged eyewitness, the cashier, found me guilty with a recommendation for mercy—which caused old Judge Lorraine K. Mix to sentence me to life in Eddyville Prison.

After I'd been in prison about four years, the Inman Company cashier who'd been the only witness against me, was himself put in jail for embezzling their funds and it came out that at the time of my arrest he had identified two other men as being the "gunman inside the office" during the payroll robbery that I was convicted of—thing was, those two guys had solid standup alibis, and I didn't.

Still later, former baseball commissioner A. B. "Happy" Chandler promised some good Christian friends of mine that if he were elected governor he would appoint his brother Earl Chandler to personally investigate my case. After ole "Happy" was elected Governor, based on his brother Earl Chandler's thorough investigation of my case and his recommendations regarding it, true to his word (as most "down home" Kentucky people are), Governor Chandler ordered the Parole Board to release me.

For the next several years, during which I was never arrested for even a minor traffic violation, I owned and operated gaming concessions on various shows, such as, Rod Link's "World of Pleasure Shows," Jerry Wisdom's "Forsythe & Dowis Show," Punk Hill's "Hill's Greater Shows," Junior Schradier's "Broadbeck & Schradier Shows," Pete Seabrand's "Seabrand Brothers' Circus & Carnival," and played numerous state fairs, including Frontier Days at Cheyenne, Colorado State Fair at Pueblo, the New Mexico State Fair at Albuquerque, the Arizona State Fair at Phoenix, the Mid-South Fair in Memphis and the big Texas State Fair at Dallas.

I quit the carny in 1962 and became half owner of an after hours club named "The Venus Cafe" in San Francisco. A jealous hardcase named "Tough Tony" Jockamo, who owned "The Three J's" and "The Silver Saddle" tried to put me and my partner Merritt Snyder out of business. It didn't work. Later, however, after I'd sold my share of the club to Merritt and moved to Las Vegas, one of Jockamo's bartenders shot and killed Merritt.

My wife Ruby and I went to Vegas where I became associated with several corporations, namely as president of David Rose Enterprises, an original arts leasing firm; president of G.R.C., Inc., a softwares and commercial laundry equipment leasing company; as a director of U-Lease, Inc., an automobile leasing firm; and as a director in Myron MacPeck's MacPeck Realty, Ltd.

In April of 1965, while a director of the Guardian Memorial Foundation of Kansas City, Missouri, I was jumped by eight F.B.I. men while attending a businessmen's luncheon at the Holiday Inn in Kansas City, Kansas, and erroneously charged with being one of two gunmen who had robbed the Giant Food Mart in Fresno, California, on October 14, 1964—and in escaping, apparently the gunmen had temporarily "kidnapped" one Donald Mark Teeter.

In July of 1965 I was forcefully extradited to Fresno, a town I'd never been in before in my life and charged with armed robbery and kidnapping. Kidnapping in the state of California carries four sentences: simple kidnapping is 1-to-25 years, kidnapping with violence or injury to the "victim" is life, life without possibility of parole or death in the state's gas chamber.

So, not being guilty and therefore having to plead not guilty and stand jury trial, I found myself at the age of thirty-five facing the death penalty once more in a state court for a crime I had not committed! Nearly ten years have passed now. I have had two jury trials, been reversed via the Fifth District Court of Appeals twice, affirmed by the California State Supreme Court once, had a writ of certiorari denied by the United States Supreme Court, been denied my application for pardon by Governor Ronald Reagan, been twice denied my application for parole by the Adult Authority and presently have a writ of habeas corpus before federal judge Myron D. Crocker in Fresno and a petition for pardon to the Adult Authority for Governor Edmund G. Brown, Jr.

As you can see I've been pretty busy legally as a lifer in Folsom Prison, but I've managed to do a few other things also, like: being elected to nine terms as Chairman of the Folsom's Creative Writers' Workshop, earning a High School Diploma from the Folsom Cordova Unified School District, earning a Diploma from the Central Bible College of Springfield, Missouri, under the direction of Chaplain Russell Knight, earning seven Certificates of Completion from the Salvation Army Bible Study Division under Major Charles Griffin, was awarded two Certificates of Appreciation by the Beth Israel Congregation of Sacramento by Rabbi Joseph J. Ehrenkrantz, earning three awards from the Department of Journalism of the Southern Illinois University at Carbondale for outstanding reportage on the Folsom *Observer* (am the former Editor and now Sports Editor) and am a published poet who has written over 2,500 poems, composed some 50 hymns and written the lyrics to approximately 150 country and western songs. I am also a man who spends many frustrated nights in my too small cell contemplating the sworn affidavits and wondering *when* the TRUTH will set me FREE again.

DIALOGUE CONVICT

Joe Convict

A conversation between a "free person" and an old convict that has done (too) much time:

FREE PERSON: I've heard so many people, free and convict alike, knock the justice system, but I have yet to see a comprehensive *constructive* suggestion as to how the system *should* work; what actual changes should be made?

JOE CON: You mean a *real* system of justice?

FP: Yes!

JC: Man, you're talking about a whole *lot* of change!

FP: That bad?

JC: *Worse!* You're talking about changing the complete concept of thinking of a whole nation. There are over 200 million people out there that have had their thinking warped by *centuries* of propaganda put out by "public relations" departments (funded by the public's tax dollars) of hundreds of bureaucracies whose only goal is to justify their own existence and to perpetuate and guarantee their own jobs. You're also talking about doing away with, or greatly reducing the size of, many of these bureaucracies. This last is a formidable task. When people are fighting for their existence, they can get *vicious*.

FP: I don't understand your linking "public relations" and propaganda.

JC: Most people don't. That's why the name on the door says *Public Relations*—to misguide the taxpayers who are paying for the whole thing. Over the years I've watched the press releases gush out of those "public relations" departments, full of self-justification, full of words that *sound* nice but mean something else, or full of out-and-out lies. Their jobs are made much simpler nowadays because the news media doesn't look *into* stories; they just accept and print press releases. The paradox is that the taxpayers are paying the complete bill for the system that is misleading them and keeping them ignorant.

FP: Why don't the convicts have a voice?

JC: A good question; one I'd like to see answered by (1) the California Department of Corrections (CDC) who won't allow newspeople free access to prisons, (2) newspeople who don't make more than a token effort to talk to prisoners and who accept the dictates of prison officials excluding them from prisons, (3) the legislature or the judges who won't pass a law or issue a court order allowing news media free access to the prisons. Ideally convicts should be allowed to fund their *own* "public relations" bureau from the multimillion dollar Inmate Welfare Fund (money taken from convicts).

FP: If the money is theirs, why couldn't they do that?

JC: The money *is* theirs, but it was taken from them without their permission and it's controlled by the CDC; who decides how the money is to be spent (usually on items that are then labeled "privileges," that can be taken away for "misbehavior"). Another thing IWF money could be used for is to hire a legislative lobbyist for convicts.

FP: Why should convicts have a lobbyist?

JC: To counterattack the efforts of *several* lobbyists who are in effect *anticonvict*.

FP: *Anticonvict* lobbyists?

JC: That's right. The CDC has one. The CSEA (California State Employees Association) has one. The CCOA (California Correctional Officers Association) has one. These men represent the interests of the CDC or the employees thereof. Their interests are almost always in conflict with those of the convicts. Check any penal reform bill and then note the position taken by those organizations. Their lobbyists are busy defeating or making crippling amendments to any penal reform bill.

FP: Do those organizations have that much power?

JC: Let me give you a little example of something that really happened. Back during 1970–1971 the CDC went through a rare short period of sanity wherein a lot of men were being paroled and the prison population dropped to 16,000 men. *Some* people in penology rejoiced. Here was a chance to *close* several prisons, for a savings of millions of dollars of the taxpayers' money. The newspapers happily spread the news of the pending closure of "the pit" (San Quentin) and of the "Conservation Center" at Susanville. Marin County never has appreciated the ugly cancer in its side at Point San Quentin. The per capita income in Marin County is high. The money generated by the prison wouldn't be missed there. But in Susanville it *would!* Isolated up in the hills, the logging and farming industry gone bad, the town of Susanville panicked. Not thinking or caring about the 1,350 men whose freedom they'd be jeopardizing, the people of that community were only concerned with the nice million-dollar cushion that brick monstrosity outside of town represented. The ex-farmers were now Gentlemen Farmers, "working" their eight hours as a guard, driving their brand new $5,000 four-wheel drive pickups; concerned only about their new horse trailers which carried their registered riding horses. Suddenly they *were* concerned about *losing* this bit of easy-pickings. Organizations were formed. Businessmen panicked. A deluge of letters descended on Sacramento. Pressure was brought to bear on the legislature and other politicians. The possible closing of two prisons, with the attendant threat of loss of jobs created a stir in the CCOA. Members kicked in *$50 apiece* to a fund to prevent the closure of the prisons.

Then the strangest things happened. Someone suddenly decided that Susanville would make a lovely "Vocational Training Center" although it was designed and built to function, as a minimum security conservation camp center. Reasons mysteriously appeared as to why San Quentin couldn't be closed.

This created another problem. Susanville was almost half empty. San Quentin was down to less than 2,000 men (the south block holds *that* many). Another strange thing happened! Our illustrious Governor Ronald Reagan discovered a sudden overwhelming need to "protect the public" from all these monster convicts. The parole board was "called in" and told to immediately initiate a "get tough" policy. The following year 5,000 fewer paroles were granted. 5,000 men arbitrarily lost their freedom; not because of their crimes, but for political expediency.

Susanville is now full. San Quentin's population has doubled. Of course, everyone there has to be kept locked in their cells all the time. For some reason they're angry and violent. The correctional officers are happy though. Jobs are no longer in danger (there are over 23,000 men in prison now . . . more than in the *whole* U.S. federal prison system). CDC is now even hiring *more* guards (have to control the violence, you know). That's alright, the taxpayers will foot the bill.

FP: All that? Sounds pretty hard to believe!

JC: Check it out! It's all been documented. Go back and check the newspapers. The parts they wouldn't publish can be *proven* by prison reform groups like the Prisoners' Union in San Francisco and the Committee for Prisoner Humanity and Justice in San Rafael.

FP: Just to protect a few hundred jobs?

JC: A few hundred very cushy jobs, with few requirements. Suppose you were suddenly told to find new jobs for several hundred ex-cops, ex-prison guards, and ex-parole board members. Where would you place them?

FP: A tough question. Hmmm! How about the military?

JC: That's where most of them *came* from. Now, think about this: If given a little bit of help (plus a *chance*) most convicts *have* a trade they could use to earn a living.

FP: You're making me wonder just *who* is the parasite on the taxpayers' dollars!

JC (big smile): So, you see, *that* would be the biggest problem of all. If someone, somewhere, could just figure out a way to give jobs to thousands of ex-cops, ex-prison guards, ex-parole board members, etc., it would be *easy* to change the justice system. If that can't be done, those thousands will be viciously opposing you, all the way!

FP: Well, let's just make a little supposition here and say some genius could find jobs for all the above ex's, what else has to be done?

JC: The first thing that has to be done is some more supposing. We're going to have to suppose that it wouldn't take an intensive publicity campaign for many years to get all the nonsense *out* of people's heads that is now *in*. Then we're going to have to suppose that the individual states would allow their state's-rights perogative to be modified to allow a *national* penal code. The third supposition is that everybody would agree to let one man set up the new "justice system." Here it will have to be me since you have put me in the spot (supposition-wise).

FP: You think it would have to be delegated to *one man?*

JC: Did you ever try to get a group of humans to agree on *anything?*

FP: Okay! I delegate *you*. But, why a *national* penal code?

JC: We're back to the same old thing. The individual states would fight ratification. They'd want to change *this*, or *that*. We'd end up back where we are now. It's either that, or limit this to *one* state.

FP: Okay, you're in charge. Set up a National Penal Code.

JC: The first thing to be done is to weed out the garbage; things that shouldn't be crimes.

FP: Such as?

JC: Moral crimes. It's not the function of government to legislate morality.

There should be only *one* sex crime; a law against any- one forcing someone to do something against their will. (Child molesting would be considered a *mental* problem and treated as such.)

Prostitutes would be licensed. The only restriction being that they get periodic checks by a doctor. They would pay taxes and *contribute* to the economy instead of costing the taxpayers money.

Indecent exposure is a mental problem.

Next comes a non-crime that will be opposed by *other* elements. At least two that I can think of: the State of Nevada and the Mafia.

FP: Gambling?

JC: Yup. Nevada would have to make itself attractive to industry *or something*.

The Mafia would be a *large* problem. I would be stepping on their corns all over the place. I already removed the whores from their payroll, now comes gamb- ling, next goes dope. Under my system the Mafia would be in deep trouble. They'd have to take all their money and *really* go into legitimate business, or move their operations to some stupid country that is like ours *used* to be (one that fosters ridiculous conditions that *create* crime so that the slick ones can make money either breaking the unnatural laws or pretending to try to enforce them). We'll have to *suppose* that we somehow got around the Mafia problem and the many politicians they own.

Gambling would be wide open, except that the government would control the major types. The money from gambling would allow taxes to be greatly reduced.

(A thought: Maybe all our ex's could be put to work for the government in the gambling industry, in positions where they couldn't abscond with the money!)

Next come narcotics. Why should the government care who uses dope? If we want to get moralistic, we can put a warning on the label like we do on cigarettes (which cause cancer) and like we should require on booze (which causes all kinds of tragic mental and physical problems). Do you realize how many *billions* of dollars are spent every year trying to enforce narcotics laws?

Marijuana would be legal. *Tiajuana Gold* could be a brand name. There would be a warning on the pack: Danger! Marijuana may make you giggle. Packets of seeds could be sold by Burpee Seed Co.

Most people aren't aware that users of heroin (and other drugs) could lead a functional life, hold a job, etc., if they weren't *forced* into becoming a criminal. How many people reading this could come up with $50 to $100 a day extra? This is the amount of money our laws force these people to pay for their narcotics. A small percentage of these people can legally make enough money to pay that price. A large percentage *sells* enough dope to pay for their own. The rest (some 60% to 70%) have to *steal* $50 to $100 a day. Most of these *forced* thieves don't steal cash. They have to steal merchandise and then they sell the merchandise for about one-fifth its value. That means that *each* user has to steal $250 to $500 worth of property *every day*. (I'm sure glad *I'm* not a dope-fiend; I don't know *how*

I could steal that much stuff.) That's why your color TV and stereo aren't safe in your own home. You also pay inflated prices in stores to cover merchandise lost to shoplifting. Can you see how our so-called "moral" laws *create* crime?

My system would set up clinics all over the country where registered addicts could buy the amount of dope they need for its *real* price; about what most people pay for a pack of cigarettes.

The whole system of clinics, etc., could be established in about six months. The *immediate* aftereffect would be a drop in crimes involving property loss that would probably be about 60% to 70%.

FP: That's a pretty large drop in crime!

JC: Isn't it? And all we'd have to do would be to allow a few thousand people the right to use narcotics if they wanted to.

FP: What about these overdoses we always hear about?

JC: Those are usually caused by different strengths of dope according to how much each seller "cuts" it. My system would make available "laboratory grade" stuff. Users would have to be cautioned how much to use at first, until they got used to it. Then they'd *know* how much they were buying.

FP: What about these people that sell dope to kids?

JC: Society couldn't condone that. There would be laws against that just as there are laws against selling them cigarettes or booze.

Another restriction would have to be placed on its use while driving. The same restriction would apply to booze. This would have to be strictly enforced.

FP: Why do you emphasize strict enforcement on that particular area?

JC: Because I consider this one of the sick paradoxes that exist in this country. A majority of this country's "citizens" will rise up on a millisecond's notice to espouse the death penalty for the "dirty murderer" that is foul enough to take another person's life. They want him swiftly executed (as long as *they* don't have to participate in the execution). The paradox is that something like 75% of the automobile-caused deaths in this country are caused by intoxicated drivers. (The total number of these deaths, by the way, are something like *ten times* the number of deaths caused by homicide.) Yet when those same citizens mentioned previously are approached on the subject of a heavy crackdown on drunken drivers they start backing away and mumbling excuses. Why? Because a good percentage of them realize that this particular aspect of the law would focus on *them*. This can't be allowed! Don't mess with *their* little excesses!

Alcohol was once against the law. Prohibition, it was called. During that era, the whole nation thumbed their noses at "law and order." Everybody went to their favorite speakeasy. The police pretended they didn't know about it (unless they missed their weekly payoff). Millions of dollars were made by bootleggers. (This was one way our nation's "system of justice" helped organized crime get its start. After prohibition was repealed the money made from booze financed the expansion of organized crime into other "illegal activities"—moral crimes like gambling, prostitution, and narcotics.)

The government finally realized they made a mistake on prohibition and repealed it. (Too many people like booze. It's famous as "the poor people's narcotic.") The "justice system" followed the same path as organized crime and began building their bureaucracies around the "moral crimes." In the 1920s *one man*, using the taxpayers' money, conducted a long and intensive publicity campaign to convince the American public of the terrible menace presented by narcotics. (Most people aren't aware that marijuana was once quite legal in this country and that things like opium and its derivatives could be bought at the corner drugstore.) That one man *created* the narcotics

mystique in this country and *most* people *still* believe it.
That man built a nationwide bureaucracy in this country
which is now known as the Drug Enforcement Administration. The stupidity that results from all this costs the U.S.
taxpayers *billions and billions* of dollars every year,
supports *thousands* of police.

The artificially induced value of the "illicit" drugs has
created worldwide criminal syndicates to grow, smuggle,
process, smuggle, refine, smuggle, and distribute and sell
their product. This whole thing has grown to such propor-
tions that the U.S. government is threatening foreign
nations (such as Turkey) to force them to stop growing
opium poppies, etc. We've spent millions of dollars to
partol the 1,500 mile U.S./Mexican border. We supply
arms and helicopters to the Mexican government so that
the *federales* can swoop down on some poor farmer in the
state of Guerrero to murder him with machineguns and
burn his marijuana crop.

All this sickness is then reported over the boob-tube to
the American public and they sit in ignorant bliss and nod
their heads in amazement at the wonderful job that "law
enforcement" is doing to prevent the spread of this
"terrible menace."

When this ignorant bliss is jarred to a state of reality by
the splintering crash of their front door being torn loose
from its hinges and shotguns jammed under their noses,
they watch in terror as self-righteous fanatics tear the
privacy of their home to shreds. They breathe a sigh of relief as someone shows up "a few minutes late" to inform
this gang of madmen that they're on the wrong block. It's
only after Joe Citizen is left alone to try to put the house
back together that he begins to realize his "rights" have
been violated. Fear is replaced by anger. The next day he
learns that the U.S. government has somehow bypassed
the U.S. Constitution and has passed what they call a "no-
knock law."

What they don't hear about is the poor hippie, with the

peace symbol hanging from his neck, who moved way off into the mountains to get away from this madness, to be alone with his woman, to smoke a little pot or to drop a little acid, who ran in fear when a helicopter landed in his yard and a gang of men leaped out with shotguns, who died from multiple shotgun wounds because of the above-mentioned sins.

FP: Whooee!

JC: Sorry about that. Sometimes I get a little wound-up on this subject.

FP: After all that, who could blame you?

JC: The people in the "justice system" who are wrapped up in all this and who, sadly, believe their own propaganda and really believe they're doing what's right.

FP: What could be done about all this?

JC: Aside from a nationwide epidemic of common sense, the only alternative I can see is many years and millions of dollars spent to counterattack propaganda with *truth*. Perhaps that might induce some common sense in the human animal so that he might quit *creating* a lot of the sickness that exists in this world.

FP: We've kind of wandered off the track. Are there any more moral crimes?

JC: No, I guess that pretty well covers it.

Next I want to talk about crimes of violence. Now, when I say "crimes of violence," I refer to actual incidents of *physical harm* perpetrated on one person by another. There is no room in this category for such idiotic phrases as "psychological violence," "threatened violence," or the ultimate stupidities "implied, or *potential* violence."

This is the one category that leaves me puzzled. No civilized society can allow violence to exist unchecked in its midst. Violent people are, luckily for most of us, in a small minority. If allowed to exist unchecked, this minority could make life miserable for the majority of us that can coexist *without* violence. This minority is compelled to resort to violence because of whatever it is that's lacking in their personality that prevents them from relating and co-existing without it. I have a tendency to relegate this into the psychological area. Not having that much knowledge of psychiatry, I don't know if there is a *cure*, per se. Like most people, I have a strong aversion to the *Clockwork Orange* syndrome; invasions, destructions, or control mechanisms upon a person's brain. Having seen, and being strongly aware of, the inherent abuses in this type of thing, I fervently reject it.

Also included with the above category (because I can't think of anywhere else to put them) are *non*violent "crimes against a person," such as: kidnapping, holding a captive, child-stealing, and other such crimes against a person (*without* actual, perpetrated violence) which society can't tolerate.

These are the only categories of crime for which I can see no alternative but imprisonment. The problem is that since there seems to be no "cure," what will imprisonment accomplish (except isolating the violent from the non-violent)? I have seen, and been subjected to, the isolation technique of "crime prevention," so therefore, I'm well aware that it doesn't perform any constructive service. If the psychiatric field can't come up with any socially accep-table method of treatment, I'm at a loss for any construc-tive suggestion here.

Some thought might be given to a "penal community"; a complete living area that is isolated by an impenetrable security perimeter. The violence prone could be isolated in a community of their peers to iron out their problems and to live as normal an existence as they allow each other.

The possible exception would be the so-called "crimes of passion"; the isolated instances of homicide, etc., in which experience has shown that this type of person acts out once and thereafter is a "model citizen" both during imprison-ment and after release. For this type of crime society could figure out how many years of vengeance it feels compelled to require (I would suggest 5 to 7 years), place these men with their own kind in whatever type of penal setting is required until they finish their "term," and then set them free (with post-release help).

In the rare instance of an incorrect classification in which a second incident of violence occurs with an individual, off with them to the "Violence Colony."

FP: I like that idea about a "penal colony."

JC: Yes, it's usable as a last resort. I used to think that would be a "cure" for everything—to replace prisons.

FP: What changed your mind?

JC: Experience; more exposure to ideas and experiences in the penal field and penal reform.

FP: Now you have something better?

JC: I think so. Now we come to the area of crime in which there is the most *real* criminal activity, and which requires the most diversified programming: "money or property" crime. This is where actual property or money is taken. Under my system, imprisonment or restraint of freedom would be the *last* possible consideration here. A man would almost have to insist on having his freedom restricted. The system would be structured in steps, all directed toward restitution. After a trial to prove his guilt, a hearing would be had to determine the value of the property lost or damaged; also a value-penalty for inconvenience or deprivation.

A man would be placed in Phase One if he was never-before-convicted, or if his past record indicated he could be trusted to conform to Phase One conditions. Phase One would remain free in the community with the condition that he maintain employment and make payments toward restitution until he paid back the amount that was decided on at the restitution hearing. Upon completion of the payments he would be free. The main requirement for Phase One would be that the individual have a paying job or trade where he could immediately go to work and remain employed until he paid off his debt.

The latter requirement would also apply to Phase Two, except Phase Two would be required if the offender was irregular in his payments, had a minor alcoholic (or other) problem that interfered with his job performance, or if he was convicted of additional thefts while in Phase One. Phase Two would consist of a work-furlough-type system where a man lived in a work-furlough center at night and was released every day to go to work. He would be required to turn in his checks, would receive weekly expenses, would pay a room-and-board charge, and the rest of his money would be kept in an account for him (returnable upon his release).

An alternative in Phase Two might be for a man to sign himself into a Penal Cooperative (a system similar to the Delancey Street operation in San Francisco, wherein a group has several businesses of their own in which their members work). The Penal Cooperative would keep the man's salary (except for his daily expenses), pay off the man's debts, deduct living expenses, and when he left he would have an accumulated savings to start with.

If a man were unable to acquire a job or had no skills, an industrial training program would be available to him from private industry (who would be recruited into this program through contracts with the state). The offender would be paid an hourly wage for his participation, which would increase with his skills and effort. The offender would participate in this program on a Phase One or Two basis according to the standards already applied.

There should be a similar vocational training program, if the man's talents or desires made him lean more towards a trade. The problem here is how the man makes money to earn a living and to pay his restitution. This might be solved by a government-financed program of grants or loans. (A loan could be repaid out of future earnings.)

Phase Three would come into effect when: (a) a man

would just flat refuse to participate in any of the previous programs, or if (b) he attempted to elude restitution by packing his belongings and pulling a disappearing act. Phase Three would also consist of an industrial training program (with private industry on a contract basis), but would have a penal-colony-type security area built adjacent to the industrial training facility. Category (a) from above would be *sentenced* there; so would (b) when caught and returned. These offenders would be required to work (at a wage comparable to outside work) in the industrial facility, to pay their room and board, to pay their restitution, and to perhaps accumulate a small nest egg before their release. The ones from category (b) would also be required to pay for reasonable court and transportation costs incurred in returning them from their flight. Proper safeguards would have to be set up in this program to prevent its degeneration into a slave-labor camp, and to keep living conditions in the security area as free from repression as possible.

Phase Four would, regrettably, probably be necessary for the hard-nosed few that just wouldn't have anything to do with the aforementioned programs. This would have to be a lockup-type place. Only one small one would be required for a whole state. About the only way to handle this would be to place a value of so-many-dollars-a-day on the time spent in there (adding in room-and-board costs). The men would be released when the proper amount of days had "paid" for their debt.

FP: That sounds like a pretty sensible solution for crimes that you can place a value on. It insists that only the "value" be replaced. It reinforces the "work ethic," yet provides help for those unable to get into the work force. The only restrictions are self-imposed. I like it!

JC: Thank you! Something else it does is to eliminate the "crime school" effect, wherein present offenders learn how to be "better criminals."

FP: You're right, I didn't think of that!

JC: There are a few other minor areas of "crime" I haven't covered. I'll go through them quickly. Destruction of property, or vandalism. These offenders would, if at all possible, be required to repair the damage with their own physical labor, paying for the materials necessary. If the damage is too extensive for that, the problem would be taken care of the same as a "property" crime.

Then would come the "violation of rules" type thing. Innovative sentencing would be encouraged here as much as possible, such as: If a person allowed their dog to defecate on a public sidewalk, they would be required to clean up so-many of the offending objects. A litterbug would be required to pick up so-much litter.

FP: Yeah, that does make sense.

JC: If innovative sentencing couldn't be applied, fines could be used.

FP: What about the type of crimes that are now called "aggravated" crimes; like robbery with violence, or possesion of a gun while committing a crime?

JC: "Multiple offense" crimes will be treated as if each offense were a separate crime. Robbery with violence would be charged as (a) a robbery (first- or second-degree according to how it was perpetrated), and (b) violence, according to what type of violence occurred. Evidence would be considered during the trial and the final decision would be up to the jury to decide (within the limits set by law). Violence (if proven) would take precedence over anything else. As stated before, this would mandate shipment to the "Violence Colony." Offenders would soon get the message, and they would avoid the aggravation of crimes by violence.

FP: What about the possession of a gun while committing a crime?

JC: My system wouldn't penalize anyone for mere *possession* of something.

FP: You mean if a man was convicted of a crime, nothing would be said if he had a gun on him when he was arrested?

JC: A gun is a piece of metal. Why should a person be punished for having a piece of metal in his pocket?

FP: But he could have *killed* somebody!

JC: So could you every time you take your car out on the street. A car is several thousand pounds of metal. Traveling at 50 mph, that's quite a lethal weapon!

FP: But a gun was *designed* to kill people!

JC: A gun was designed to propel a piece of lead a certain distance at a certain speed. The *vast majority* of guns are used to plunk holes in pieces of paper (targets) or in tin cans. Some are used to kill animals (something I consider a sickening aspect of human nature). A very small percentage of guns are used to kill or injure people (excluding war, another sickening aspect of human nature). But the *gun* did not kill a person. If left to its own devices a gun would just lie there until it rusted to pieces. A *person* uses the gun to kill or injure someone else. If he *does*, punish him for the sickness in *him* that made him commit the act. If he didn't, then common sense should tell us that our system of laws has functioned correctly in that it shaped his attitudes toward *not* using the gun to hurt someone.

FP: Well, yes, I guess I'll have to agree with that; but don't you think that since guns can be used to kill people, that carrying them around in public should be discouraged?

JC: In comparison to how long man has been around, guns have been in existence a comparatively short time. History offers ample evidence that man killing man is not a phenomenon that suddenly materialized at the same moment the first gun was created. Before guns men killed each other very efficiently using arrows, spears, swords, knives, clubs, rocks, tree limbs—in fact, anything they could get their grubby hands on. *Because* of laws banning weapons certain Oriental societies have even developed a very efficient system of killing each other with their bare hands.

Carrying your premise of outlawing possible lethal weapons to its ultimate extreme, mankind would not only be prohibited from carrying anything in his hands, but you might also have to amputate the *hands* since *they* can be made into pretty efficient weapons.

I submit that the efforts (and laws) of society should be directed toward eliminating the detrimental effects our social interactions have on each other so that the sickness in the minds of man that make him *want* to kill or harm someone else no longer exists. One way to do this is to create a system of laws that attempts to encourage an alienated person to find a working place *in* society, not to make him *further* alienated or to create a condition where he is *less* able to cope than he was before; not by making laws that *create* crime and *make* a man into a criminal.

FP: Okay, you've convinced me.

JC: I wish it were that easy. I hope that by viewing your *own* reactions you can see how our society has been brain-washed into believing there is reason for all these millions of suppressive laws. The people in the so-called justice system seem (in the majority) to be of the mentality that believes that in order to cure something all you have to do is put a penalty on it. My personal belief is that a lot more could be accomplished by setting up laws that provide *incentive* for improved behavior.

FP: Well, your system seems to do *that* pretty well. Do we have any more categories of crime to deal with?

JC: No, that pretty well takes care of it. With minor revisions and detail-polishing what I've set up should cover most crime.

FP: Hmm, from my limited knowledge of the present system it seems a lot less complicated than what we've got.

JC: Oh yes, it's definitely simpler. I think simplicity is the essence of solving most problems.

FP: I agree with that! Do you suppose we could go back and get a quick sort of capsule review of your whole system so that I could better grasp it, in its entirety?

JC: Sure! Let's look at it from a cost analysis basis; money saved and extra money earned.

Money saved:

   A. The narcotics thing eliminated.

      a. This alone would save the U.S. taxpayers *billions* of dollars a year now spent trying to enforce these ridiculous laws.

      b. The immediate huge reduction in "property loss" narcotics related crimes would make most people more secure in their homes and safer on the streets. The price of goods in stores would go down. Store owners could reduce their security forces. Insurance costs would go down. (I'm not sure the insurance companies would be too happy about all this. Their profits would drop. They might even *oppose* these changes.)

   B. The police would *not* be:

      a. paying anyone to peek in our windows to check on what positions we assume while we're fornicating;

      b. running around in vans gathering up prostitutes;

      c. after organized crime (their "income areas" would be eliminated);

      d. after gamblers;

      e. after narcotics users, or swamped with narcotics related crimes.

The *extra benefit* here is that the police would then be able to concentrate their efforts on reduction of real crime and the prevention of violence. Although many people aren't consciously aware of it, our present system creates a contempt for the law and the police. Even the police, faced with this daily degradation, lose respect for the law, and sometimes even for themselves because of the positions it forces them into. (Hence, police accepting payoffs, etc.) Under my system, I believe the people would have a much greater respect for the law and the police. Even most of the offenders would be affected by this because they wouldn't be facing unnecessarily extreme penalties. There would be less fear of law and the police; therefore creating more respect for both, and since violence is *created* by fear this would greatly reduce the *incentive* for violence.

A man that knows he's going to be *helped* (except when he uses violence) won't logically *resort* to violence.

Less offender violence would affect the public in that they would be less likely to react to situations in a violent manner. This *could* cause a chain reaction over the whole nation with the result a deemphasis on violence.

FP: Sounds logical. I know this sounds out-of-place here, but I've got a picture in my mind of a possible situation where (under your system) a man might commit a crime just to *get* help.

JC: Quite possible. Along those lines, here are a couple of things to look at: (a) Did it ever occur to you that *now* when a man commits a crime it's often a cry for help? And, believe me, that's the *last* thing he gets! (b) Assuming your above situation, if a man *did* have that in mind he sure wouldn't do anything serious, and he'd do it with the knowledge and intent that he would be paying restitution for his crime. Can the same be said of our present system?

If it was intended to *prevent* such a situation from occurring, it could be made possible for a man to *volunteer* himself for the industrial or vocational training programs, either under Phase One or Two conditions. Can you think of a *better* means of crime prevention?

FP: No, I can't. An excellent idea!

JC: Back to money saved:

      C. The city and county jails wouldn't be packed because we've eliminated whores, narcotic and narcotic-related crimes, and "restitution" cases. Fewer jails would be needed. A lot of bad ones could be closed.

D. Only a few (small population) prisons would be needed:

   a. a "Violence Colony";
   b. a place for "Crimes of Passion";
   c. Phase Four—a place to "sit out" a fine or restitution penalty at so-much money per day (an unused county jail could probably be utilized for this);
   d. Phase Three (built next to an industrial training facility). There would be a *huge* amount of money saved here. California's taxpayers give up over $200 million a year to support its 17 prisons.

E. Many unnecessary jobs would be eliminated (those mentioned in the very beginning that we *supposed* somebody could find legitimate employment for):

   a. vice squad (men infamous for *their* sexual oddities);
   b. the Federal Narcotics Enforcement Administration bureaucracy;
   c. all the state narcotics cops;
   d. the many narcotics undercover cops and informers;
   e. probably some judges, since the court calendars would suddenly get *un-jammed;*
   f. all the *penocrats:*
      1. prison guards (California taxpayers have to pay approximately $134 million a year to support theirs);
      2. prison and department of corrections administrators;
      3. prison "counselors" (a man that a convict talks to for half an hour per year);

4. parole board members (California's 25 demigods cost the state's taxpayers over a million dollars a year—$680,000 in salaries alone);

5. parole and probation officers (there would be no parole or probation officers since there would be no parole or probation);

6. the multitude of clerks, secretaries, etc. this is the one category of prison-related employees that could find employment elsewhere; there's always a need for typing, filing, etc.).

F. Since the court calendars wouldn't be jammed with cases, all the varied expenses saved here would be less money out of the taxpayers' pockets.

FP: Sounds like we've saved a *whole bunch* of money!

JC: In California it would be hundreds of millions. Nationwide it would add up to *billions!* Do you suppose that might ease our "National Debt"?

FP: Most definietly! Plus we'd all be paying a lot less income tax.

JC: Right! The nice thing about most of these programs is that they would pay their own way. Some of them might require an initial expense, but that would be more than paid for by the substantial savings mentioned previously. An *extra benefit* is that a lot of crime victims would be receiving restitution. This would be accomplished through the program and not by using *public* money as is now done in the few such systems that do exist. And I haven't even mentioned the *extra income* these programs would produce.

FP: *Extra* income?

JC: Yup. Look at all the people that would be paying taxes that now aren't: (a) organized crime (their old "income areas" eliminated, they would now be paying income tax because they wouldn't have to hide their new income); (b) whores would be paying taxes (they make pretty big money, too); (c) all the men on "restitution status" would be paying taxes.

There would naturally be taxes on marijuana, just as there is on tobacco—*more* income.

Last, but not least, is the money the government would make from their control of gambling. If this didn't completely *eliminate* income tax, it should come close.

One of my favorite ideas is to set aside enough money out of the gambling take to support the nation's education system. This in turn would allow a complete *elimination* of property taxes on private land. This would enable the government to return something they stole from our citizens; something that used to be very basic to our whole society.

FP: What's that?

JC: A citizen's sovereignty over his own land. It used to be in this country that if a person works hard all his life to pay for a piece of land and a home, it was *his*. Nobody could take it away from him. Nowadays, everybody has to pay the government rent (in the form of taxes) for the privilege of living on their own land. If they don't, government takes it away from them. That isn't right.

FP: I'm with you all the way on that point!

JC: There are a great many changes that have to be made in the whole arrest-to-sentencing procedures, but since we've run up against space and time problems we won't be able to go into them at this time. Perhaps some other time.

FP: Too bad we have to cut it short. Do you think there is much hope for such extensive reform?

JC: As long as our current situation exists, no! The people now in power feel secure by perpetuating the current system. We *must*, however, get rid of the indeterminant sentencing system and its attendant parole boards. Any time you have a situation where a great deal of leeway is allowed for human discretion, *abuse* of that discretion will be standard policy. The best thing that can be done now is to set up a system of *exact* penalties for specific crimes, penalties that *aren't* excessive (despite public pressure that often prompts legislators into such action). Excessive penalties have been proven to be ineffective. They just creat hostility and make the situation worse.

There is a good law now pending in the California Legislature that would create the above situation in that state. (SB 42 by Senator Nejedly.) The bill was almost killed last year because of squabbling among the many people concerned. If all these people would just quit worrying about feeding their *own little egos* and get together and *pass the bill,* it would be a great step in correcting the many abuses inherent in the present system. Almost *anything* is an improvement over what we've now got!

I'VE DONE IT AGAIN

Preston Riley

I have always drunk alcohol since I can first remember. If I couldn't get it legally from someone, I'd steal it; and have been in trouble because of it almost from the first drink. Drinking, along with my rebellious ways, eventually led me to and down the inevitable creek minus a paddle.

I was always a rebel, even as a kid. My father often told me he'd live to see me in the penitentiary. He didn't quite make it. The day I was put in the county jail in northeast Arkansas for burglary and grand larceny, my uncle and some cousins came to the jail to tell me my dad and one of my brothers had drowned the day before while they were fishing down in Florida.

Most people, when they hear the names "Cummins," "Tucker," or "Arkansas State Penitentiary," automatically think of certain death, due largely to worldwide news coverage of events that happened during 1967 and 1968. Some think of it as a place where inmates were clubbed, shot, strangled, or killed in any other manner by prison officials, "Captains" as they were then called, or trustee guards known as "shotguns," "high powers," or "snakes," a term derived partly from the A.S.P., Arkansas State Penitentiary.

I had the same thoughts as most everyone else about these places when the circuit judge handed me a three-year stretch for burglary with five more suspended for grand larceny. That was October of 1967.

"I can't do no three years!" I thought. "Hell, here I've made it for 33 years without a prison record, and I'm just *too* damn old to be branded a convict now!" All these thoughts didn't do me a nickle's worth of good, though, because even though I cried, pleaded, and begged as much as I dared, the sentence was still there.

The day I went to court, I was scared to death. I could see myself dead at an age much too young to be departing from worldly pleasures. I found I had much to stay at home for, although I hadn't done too good of a job of it before I got locked up in May, five months before court. (There is only a circuit court twice a year in this part of Arkansas, and I had just barely missed the spring court by a week or so, so I had to stay in jail until the fall session.)

I had a new baby son, barely eight-months old, when I went to court, and thoughts of him and his mother visiting me in the jury box, where they let them visit me because there was no jury trial that day and they could keep their eyes on me all at the same time, kept running through my mind all the time I was in insolation after getting to the penitentiary. He had needed me, to my notion, much more than the state did. My wife, as most wives do at a time like this, had promised faithfulness, but since I was locked up and she knew I wouldn't be coming home these nights, I could picture different men at my house every night. Lord, Lord, jealousy sure does make for some "hard" time!

My son, who had been raising cane all through my trial and sentencing, when handed to me while visiting in the box, had decided to use my chin as a teether. He raised cane after the visit was over, being used to my chin as it was considerably longer than his mother's and more to his liking. After giving him back to his mother, I noticed that he had also used my lap for a lavatory. This didn't bother me too much, however, even though the courtroom was full of people, some with relatives on trial and some just gawkers. It wouldn't have made my son any difference, one way or another, to be sent right along to the pen with me. All these thoughts were in my head my first few days of prison life.

I arrived at the A.S.P. November 12, 1967, went through isolation, getting about five shots, plus a vaccination, and was a little better oriented to prison life by the time I was released into the population. The prison administration was being shaken up by Governor Winthrop Rockefeller at the time I was to stay at Cummins. Tucker was where most of the young offenders were sent, and also had a maximum custody facility as this was where the electric chair was. So staying at Cummins was the first of my druthers, if I was to have any druthers.

I had heard from a parole violator, who was also taking back a new beef, that the best way to get established, and in a hurry, was to single out a man, preferably a murderer or the like, and "knock fire from his ass." He said nobody would bother you after that. I decided that this was what I'd do upon my arrival at the prison. He *didn't* tell me, though, that the inmate you hit just might "creep" on you, and plant a Kaiser blade, or one of the heavy hoes they use for cutting ditch banks and chopping cotton, in your back. I heard about that shortly after getting there, while I was still in isolation, thank God, and radically changed my plans for getting established.

I had also heard from the parole violator that while you were on the long-line or garden squad, the two most common jobs upon arrival, the guards might shoot the cup out of your hand while you are getting a drink of water, or having a cup of the state-issued coffee you could buy from whatever inmate owned this product at the time.

At that time, when you first got to ASP, it was a long-standing custom to cut off all your hair, so they called new arrivals "shorthairs." In order not to give anyone the pleasure of cutting off all my hair, I shaved my head, even my eyebrows, before going to Cummins. After I got there I found it wasn't necessary to have all your hair cut off anymore, so that was another knock against my rebelliousness.

I am continuously amazed at the flexibility of man's ability to adapt to facts, and getting sent to any prison is hard fact of the first order.

I was out of isolation about a week, and getting used to the fact I was a convict, when the assistant warden, J. R. Price, called me to his office. I was looking for the worst, ready to feel the strap on my rear end. I didn't know what rule I'd broken, but knew I'd broken one, somehow. It was because one of my wife's aunts, though, had called him that day. My son had contacted meningitis, and they weren't looking for him to live.

This was a desperate situation for me, because he had been taken to a hospital in Memphis, Tennessee and, this being out of state, a leave of emergency was ruled out. I began immediately to make plans to escape. Since there were no walls, I didn't figure there would be too much of an obstacle to overcome. Some of the captains, however, must have known how I felt, and saw me eyeing the highway, because they warned me I wouldn't make it.

They did, however, let me make phone calls to the people who knew how things were. They let me make them each day, in fact. And also write extra letters, as at that time there was a limit to the amount of mail you could send or receive. They did not charge me with these. A couple of the captains taking money from their pockets to mail them, but still acting tough so you didn't take it as weakness. None of the captains wanted to be tagged "soft," so they kept up their front.

I lived in a world then of several dimensions. Each day I waited for the news of my son's death, and would dream of the day in the court house, and of days before that when they would come to visit me in the county jail and he would climb all over the bars, to everyone's amusement, and yell at the top of his voice.

I lost much sleep due to this, and also due to being in a strange place where I could see all sorts of men slipping up on me with knives, hatchets, and everything that could kill you. Of course, this was only my imagination getting the best of me, and compounded due to my lack of sleep.

I finally got word from home that they didn't think my son would live through the night. So I went once again to the warden about four o'clock in the afternoon. The warden told me if he continued to get worse, they would take me to Memphis, but I would have to go in handcuffs and leg irons. He let me make another phone call home, and I found my son had improved a little, but was still under the care of a specialist.

Now I began to worry about the cost because specialists don't come cheap. I was afraid he would quit if I didn't find some way to pay him, and I had no idea how I was going to do that. Hell, I was having to smoke state-issued Prince Albert smoking tobacco. So how in the world was I going to come up with two or three thousand dollars just like that? Well, they couldn't lock me up for it, even if they wanted to, so I promised myself I wasn't going to worry about it—not just yet, anyway.

About two weeks of frustration later, I got a letter from one of my stepdaughters, a girl of thirteen who had always thought of me as her Daddy, telling me the baby was much better and would be coming home in a couple of days. Although I am not a religious man, I sat on my bunk and thanked the Lord so hard, I imagine He was glad when I turned Him loose and He could get on with His other business.

That was when life *really* started for me in the Arkansas State Penitentiary. My mind had, up until then, been so preoccupied, the long line rider, an inmate trustee, had had to call me down several times.

We were fortunate to have a good rider, an inmate trustee, because another rider might have thought I was working so hard to show the other line men up, but this one knew what I was going through because he had been told to keep a close eye on me until they could see if I was part swamp rabbit (a large rabbit that frequents the swampy parts of Arkansas, and can hit speeds in excess of thirty miles an hour, when pushed).

The rider didn't care really how much we did or didn't do, as long as it didn't reflect any laxness on his job, because riders could be strapped as easily as anyone else.

A whipping was a bad thing to see. You didn't want to look at the men getting whipped and let a captain see you, or he might say, "Since you like to watch so much, you'd probably get twice the bang out of feeling it," and lay you down with thirty or forty others, sometimes whole crews, and warm your rear with the strap, too.

I've heard rumors that they used blacksnakes and bull whips, but if they ever did, it was long before I got there.

Seeing grown men being whipped somehow seemed indecent to me, but there were some cases where it was really downright funny, too. You probably say, "How can seeing a man whipped be funny?"

Well, the truth of it is that some of the men would do things to make the captain mad on purpose, whether for contrariness or design, I'll never know, thank goodness, as I've never had that affliction!

There was one of these old " hard asses," as they were known, that everyone around got a kick out of each time he would do something, usually on purpose, to get whipped. He had a certain captain he would pick to do the strapping. He would always come off with something like, "Cap, I've got a hunnerd watt light bulb down there, an' I don't believe you can break it!"

Once when he was getting it extremely hard, he all of a sudden held up his arm and said, "Hold it, Cap!" and proceeded to lick his cigarette, light it, and then told the captain if he hadn't lost count he could continue.

Sometimes it would get the captain who was doing the whipping tickled, and he'd tell him to get up, get dressed, and go. Jesse would do it, but he'd go away acting as if he'd been cheated.

The rider on the long line would let us rest sometimes, and drink coffee (usually from pop cans with the top cut out, and a wire through a hole in the can), that you could buy for ten cents, if you happened to have it, or on credit if you had it coming. If he saw the captain coming, he would yell, "White gas!" because the captain over the long line drove a white pickup.

Our monetary system was "brozene," a hard metal made into denominations of five, ten, twenty-five, and fifty-cent pieces. There had been dollar pieces, but they were outlawed before I got there. They were dropped because of their role in gambling. It seemed like a man with a pocket full of dollar pieces couldn't rest right until he had shoved them across the poker table to someone a little luckier than he.

I was only on the long line for one month, and then went to the garage, as I had listed my occupation as a mechanic—with the acreage in cultivation we had, there was plenty of tractors, trucks, combines, hay conditioners, and what have you to break down, and some of it was down all the time.

Now I was happier, because I was doing something I liked to do. We also made extra money by working on the captain's personal cars and trucks, doing brake jobs, tune-ups, transmission overhauls, and, a few times, complete motor overhauls, until working on their vehicles was outlawed. But rules are made to apply only when a rule enforcer is present, so I made quite a bit of money on weekends when no one except the garage rider and myself were at the garage.

I changed jobs, going to heavy equipment. I dearly love listening to a big diesel engine when it's on a good steady pull, so now I couldn't be happier if I was a hog hip-deep in sour mash, and that's happy!

Christmas came and everyone got two fifty-cent brozene pieces, courtesy of a rich woman in Little Rock who had been down on prison policies for sometime. She usually gave every inmate there a dollar each Christmas.

The ASP is gone. It was replaced by the ADC, Arkansas Department of Correction; I can't say how many other changes have been made since August 1968, because that's when I was a snake no longer.

January 26, 1974, I found myself looking at prison bars again, though this time it was in another state. It is impossible to tell what goes through a person's head, or what he feels about any prison until he's there for a while. In fact, he cannot tell you himself. Fear, misgivings, apprehension, certainly all of these. He is mad and bitter, as a rule, for overlooking one small detail which had got him caught, at the police, for catching him, and the administration for not listening to what he had wanted to say because he hadn't known how to say it—mad at the word *institution* in general.

This time I found myself in Folsom Prison, in the state of California. This is another infamous prison, just as Arkansas was, except most of what I had heard about Folsom was from movies, songs and the like. I found myself comparing conditions, the system, the food, housing, and things such as the sentencing procedure of the courts, and the sentence itself.

The indeterminate sentence against the set time sentence is one of the major differences. With the indeterminate sentence, you have no certain amount of time. So, unlike serving a fixed term, for instance, five years for a burglary, or three years, such as Arkansas had given me in 1967, there is no way to earn good time. After being in a prison that gives you earned good time, being locked in one that doesn't brings a definite sense of loss—like being demoted, or going backwards instead of forwards. There is also a feeling that you are doing "dead time" if you have to wait for a board to set your time, instead of the judge who tried you. This gives you the feeling you are being tried each new time you go before the board, which, in a sense, you are. They look at your accomplishments, or demerits, and base their action on your individual case on their findings.

If these board members are ex-law enforcement officers, as I have heard, there isn't much chance of making minimum paroles. I would like to be fair to them as well as myself and say that this is *definitely* hearsay on my part.

I cannot say that I am the typical convict. I can't speak for the prison population, even in a small voice. I am an alcoholic, that really doesn't make much sense when I steal something, because at times I steal things that doesn't make any sense at all. Usually worthless things that wouldn't bring much more than the price of a beer and things I definitely cannot use. But, an alcoholic is like love. Both work in strange ways, sometimes.

Comparing food in one state institution with that of another is a contrast in itself. Institution cooks are just like moms, none cook alike, even if they cook the same things. A person likes the kind of food he is used to. If he is a southerner, as I am, he likes southern-type food. He can make fun (silently, of course!) of the way northerners, or westerners in this case, make things such as cornbread and biscuits. But, of course, this is not a cooking lesson.

Another comparison is industry versus farming. If a person was reared on a farm as I was, he is naturally more at home in an institution that farms.

Walls, as Folsom's security measure, against fences, such as Arkansas, is a change of pace in itself. Prisons are small worlds in themselves. All different, with different rules, and different personnel, with different points of view.

Bitter? No, I'm not bitter. As I said previously, I cannot say a word about other inmates points of view. I brought one number with me, and, God willing, that's the only one I'll do!

Is Folsom Prison a step backward for you? Any prison is a step backward for me, as well as most other persons. Folsom prison, by itself, is not a step backward as an institution. For those who have the time to compare such things as the indeterminate sentence to the fixed sentence, there is no comparison. This, however, is not the institution, it is the system.

I was drunk when I got to California, and was here only one day when I was picked up for burglary. Although I am not consciously making excuses for myself, I am a spur-of-the-moment criminal. To me, a crime committed in this manner is just as bad as if it was carefully planned.

I am an alcoholic which prompts these spur-of-the-moment crimes. I cannot stand to hurt anyone physically, however, the thought of killing or maiming anyone is very repugnant to me.

I was drunker than the fabled skunk when I escaped from the same county that I fell from in 1967. I escaped from this jail in October of 1973, and came to California. I had never escaped from anything before, but when drunk, any suggestion is just my meat! Too bad nobody has ever suggested joining a church while I was drunk or I may have been a Christian now instead of a convict!

THE PRISON AND I: A DESPERATE STRUGGLE

Herb Zeigler

It is impossible to make a general statement about prison because it is not so much an objective condition as it is a subjective state. Its physical reality is always thick granite walls, cyclone fences, barred windows, gun towers, bad food, raucous bells, and unvarying routine that runs into endless days and nights. But the real measure of imprisonment lies deep within the individual where he knows sadness, joy, anger, loneliness, contentment, frustration, fear, boredom, or fulfillment; and where he either rebels against the authority of the bell, the gun, and the routine or is indifferent to them.

So it is not a common experience by any means. But that's not a startling revelation, is it? Nevertheless, like the terms nigger or Jew, *convict* is a popular stereotype and as such both prison officials and the general public, all too often, assume that we all think, act and feel in the same predictable fashion.

Imprisonment, and how one deals with it, is relative, *first*, to the age, personality, character and emotional temperament of the individual. *Second,* to the nature of his crime, the anticipated length of sentence and criminal background. *Third,* to whether he has strong family and friendship ties outside. *Fourth,* to the quality of his former life, i.e. whether he was well-situated socially and economically. *And last,* to a host of other major and minor idiosyncrasies that makes one person different from another.

All of the above factors make me exclusive of every other convict on the yard, and my prison ordeal a uniquely personal condition. So this testament cannot be validated beyond the realm of my own experience. It is a feeling and interpretation that exists within me alone; I cannot presume a general convict consensus. I'm taking such precautions to emphasize this for those of you who may have a tendency to take a subjective statement and turn it into a generalized material reality, and to free myself from the ponderous responsibility of speaking for others.

Prison is a multifaceted experience and each of them demands expression; what I want to share with you is how I live and relate to these various dimensions of imprisonment. In the beginning it is like being cast in a strange dream and encountering all sorts of weird phenomena. No sooner do I deal with one than the scene changes and I'm confronted with another—then another, and another. But as in all recurring dreams I finally begin to anticipate the sequences wherein the whole experience becomes more manageable. Although I am still frightened and confused, and not at all sure it's just a dream, something inside assures me that I'm going to survive.

Public Rejection and Self-Hate

Prison is sometimes characterized as the junkyard of society. Although this description contains an element of compassion along with obvious scorn, nevertheless, they are both equally offensive to me. The term implies that I am either a mental or emotional cripple, and thereby irresponsible for my acts, or a sociopathic personality whose criminal behavior makes me morally unfit to remain in free society. Consequently, I am locked away in a steel and concrete cage until such time as I can prove my worthiness as a trusted citizen again. In the meantime my self-esteem is eroded almost to the point of nonexistence as I am persuaded to adopt the same contemptible view of myself that society has.

This taint of social and moral inferiority comes along with the conviction of the crime and echoes in the judge's words as he pronounces sentence. It is reflected in the downcast eyes of the jury, who cannot meet my gaze, to mask their shame for sitting in judgment on me. It covers me as pervasively as the ill-fitting jailhouse coveralls I wear as I am led back to the holding tank; and is reinforced by the jailer handcuffing me so tight that my hands immediately begin to swell—while he angrily glares at me as if he's society avenging angel. And it exists most decisively in the age-old concept of *penitentiary,* where I am sent to do penance, not for my sins against God, but for crimes against man.

I grew up from childhood with a strong sense of moral responsibility—of "thou shall not steal" and the Boy Scout Code of Honor, which ironically I can't recall a word of now. All this was reinforced by comic books and my favorite radio shows in which the bad guys always got caught and were justly punished for their misdeeds. And in addition, there were the whispered stories of a wayward uncle who brought shame and disgrace upon the family by constantly going to jail.

I remember quite vividly the first letter I ever wrote from captivity. I was fifteen years old and in juvenile hall for stealing a motor scooter. It was a letter to my mom, filled with heavy remorse and self-recrimination and signed *The Outcast.* I can still recall the shame and degradation. I came home singing: "Amazing grace . . . how sweet the sound that saved a wretch like me." It was my mother's favorite hymn, which impressed her no end, but unfortunately the conversion lasted only three weeks, by which time I was off and running in the streets again.

This is *only* significant when you take into consideration that it is now twenty-five years later, and during this period I've been in jail more years than I've been out. One day I found myself writing the same kind of letter again—only this time to my daughter instead of my mother. I was profusely bewailing my failure to her as a father in the same terms I'd explained my betrayal to my mom as a son—I was carrying this self-flagellation into another generation! And I determined after all these years it was a wasted trip. I have finally decided that *Amazing Grace* is not the way to personal salvation.

I admit that prison is a *junkyard* and that we should be subjected to a judicious amount of punishment, but I reject the notion that we are social and moral degenerates. Such thinking has done interminable damage to the entire prison culture and the individual striving to come to terms with himself and the world outside. It is a kind of sickness I refuse to suffer any longer.

The prison atmosphere is awash with loathing and contempt, and much of the violence we inflict upon one another is a reflection of the disgust we feel toward ourselves. Self-hate is a terrible taskmaster. It is a vile process that expresses itself even in the smallest detail of our interpersonal relationships, and until it is rooted out we will always accept the inhumanity of *the prison* as right and proper.

Crime and corruption are natural outgrowths of the American condition, and like the poor . . . "it shall be with us always." And as such I am the bastard child of a system that thrives on greed and competition while at the same time upholding symbols of honesty and virtue. It is like running a crap game—a crooked one at that—in the church basement. So I got caught with my hand in the collection plate, all right, that makes me a thief. I will accept that designation, but not proudly, because it is the last thing in the world I want to be. However, I will not accept the moral condemnation that goes with it.

I am a robber/thug/convict trapped in a world of spiritual and moral decay; I have squandered too many years in despair and self-pity which left me insensitive to the cares and concerns of the world around me. But I have discovered a new sense of myself, a value and worth that extends far beyond the walls of Folsom prison, and the recognition that salvation lies in my own personal valuation of myself—in spite of the wretchedness of my condition.

On the Rack

In spite of its sincere, but most times feeble, efforts towards rehabilitation, the primary function of prison is punishment and retribution. And that is what it does best. Punishment is in the very nature of prison itself which requires no special programs nor imaginative people to administer them. Depending on the prison and the individual's circumstances within it, punishment comes in either of two varieties: spiritual and mental anguish, or physical deprivation. Although some prisons are more pleasant than others—as their living conditions are more comparable to the military than jail—old, broken down maximum security penitentiaries such as Folsom are an abomination to both the body and spirit. And the pain of them cuts deep to the bone.

Incarceration is simply the basic stuff that punishment is comprised of, but there are a thousand-and-one, big and little things, that makes it such a bitter brew. Like: standing in the commissary line for an hour and forty-five minutes in the numbing cold or sweltering heat and have the man close the window in my face with a cheery "tough luck, buddy." Or stealing an extra cookie off the chow line and having it snatched off my tray by a snotty young bull who I'd run off the street if I ever saw him outside. Or having just finished reading *Fanny Hill* before lights outs, and the long maddening wait for my cell partner to fall asleep so I can jack off, and every time I get ready to hit it a lick he turns over and lights a cigarette. Or having had a violent argument with this same dude, who has stabbed a guy to death in another joint, makes me stay ready to jump every time he makes a move, and my fear and paranoia almost prompt me to attack him first. Or being informed that my kid brother was killed, and being allowed to call home for five minutes and having the call abruptly terminated by the Man because the time was up . . . and watching the movement sheet for the name of the dude who killed him and agonizing over what I should do if they send him here. And the pain, the insults, the frustrations continue on, and on, and on, ad infinitum . . . it is futile for me to even attempt to catalogue them. But they are there waiting for me each morning when I get up and driving me to bed each night.

American society is grossly materialistic and very often wealth is the common denominator of success, and those of us who *don't have it* are encouraged, by television and other advertising media, *to get it* by any means necessary. So until the social/political/economic system is overhauled from top to bottom, I cannot imagine an America without prisons. I acknowledge the legitimate authority of the law, the prison and all their accouterments, to protect the "legitimate" interests of society, although I hardly agree with the way they fulfill their functions. I even agree with society's need to seek vengeance against me; I cannot expect the shopkeeper to think kindly of me for ripping off his store. So in the final analysis I accept society's right to incarcerate me, and the prison's right to punish me . . . but only so far.

Punishment is a clean, innocuous-sounding word, but when applied to prison it becomes cruel, dirty and inhuman. I have seen it crush the heart and will of men who were once vibrant and alive; those who haven't the courage to commit suicide are walking around living a slow spiritual death. *Spanking* a child is sometimes a more effective corrective technique than sending him off to stand in a corner to daydream or sulk; but a *bad beating* may destroy the parent/child relationship forever. It is the same with the prisoner and the prison: the proper amount of punishment applied in the proper manner might benefit both him and society. However, when he is beaten into a miserable relic of his former self—they both lose.

Although I don't fully understand the psychology of punishment as an instrument of prison administrative policy, I know it is an external force that requires a subjective response from the individual in order to be effective. That is, at some point within himself, he can simply deny the ability of the whip to inflict pain upon him. I'm not talking about masochism—at least I hope not—nor even a perverted kind of machismo. Neither am I saying that one should embrace his imprisonment or passively accept the harsh conditions it imposes on him. There is a subtle process by which he may suspend the punitive effects of the prison if he has sufficient internal resources.

I believe, in so far as possible, that man should control the content of his own existence; this applies to convicted felons as well as to those who enjoy the highest rank and privileges of our society. And the circumstances of his existence bears very little relation to happiness and contentment or sadness and pain. After years of suffering such sorrow and pain I realized I was allowing it to happen inside me. I was responding to a preconditioned notion of what prison was supposed to be about. When you're put on the rack you're expected to cry out—even before they begin to turn the screws.

I have endured far more punishment than was justified by the meagerness of my crime. I came forth confessing my guilt and remorse, penitent and contrite, and allowed myself to be flogged through endless days and nights of incarceration. Finally I have paid. I owe nothing else to society. From this point on, the prison is in criminal violation of my sacred right *to be.*

I have retreated into a place within the center of my being, and there I have redefined myself and my circumstances and determined that I have suffered enough. Although the prison still maintains absolute control of my physical presence; even though it may still be frustrating, boring and sometimes threatening—it will never again be a pit of despair, because I am in control of my heart and spirit. Through my own will and desire I have transformed it into an affirmation of life instead of a celebration of death.

The Convict Community

The most significant element of any community is its people, it is they who give it a distinctive life and character. And so it is with prison. In spite of the walls, the guns, or the capricious authority, and regardless of the intensity of oppression, prisoners are the most dynamic force in the arrangement. Even in such bizarre conditions where they are marched lockstep to work and put on absolute silence in the mess hall, convicts still manage to sustain meaningful relationships. These relations thrive, sometimes with love and compassion, or broil over with hostility and resentment. Nevertheless, convicts are intensely involved with one another.

Lloyd McCorkle, a noted criminologist, summed up *the need* convicts have for each other, in a few succinct words: "The welfare of the individual inmate, to say nothing of his psychological freedom and dignity, does not importantly depend on how much education, recreation, and consultation he receives, but rather depends on how he manages to *live* and *relate* with other inmates who constitute his crucial and only meaningful world. It is what he experiences in this world; how he attains satisfaction from it, how he avoids its pernicious effects—how in a word, he survives in it that determines his adjustment and decides whether he will emerge from prison with an intact or shattered integrity."*

Of course this does not apply to all convicts. There are social isolates in prison just as in free society, who for one reason or another, are completely independent of the common herd. They live and breathe solely for themselves. But I am of a different nature and cannot separate my being from those around me. I cannot exist in isolation. Most likely if I were stranded in the jungle, I would take up with a troop of baboons, or even hyenas if no other life forms were available.

It may seem, by indirect reference, that I am equating convicts with animals—I have no such intention. But we are the predators of the human jungle, although many of us may have been forced to that level of existence by chance and circumstance. I am incarcerated with thieves and scoundrels of the worst sort, with robbers, rapists and murderers whose criminal histories compare with the most odious of those found in a *True Crime* magazine. But I am not appalled by their perversity nor frightened of their viciousness. Judgment is the prerogative of God alone, and each man is the only one to view his own soul.

It is among these derelicts that I have found fellowship, and a sense that each day has a special purpose even though it is limited to the cold gray walls of Folsom Prison. It is a mistake to believe that we sit twenty-four hours a day in our cells with head in hands bemoaning our transgressions against society. Although no one can tell the amount of bitter tears shed inside when we each lie down

*McCorkle, Lloyd, "Social Structure in a Prison," *The Welfare Reporter*, Vol. 8 (December 1956), p. 6.

at night, the days are consumed by the same scuffle and scurry of an ant hill. This is *real life* going on, not mere semblance, even though such crucial elements as women and children are lacking. Otherwise it contains all else we need to live and die.

It is true, a man can do years in prison without ever really becoming involved with it, but it is an empty, longing experience. It means clinging desperately to memories that grow dimmer with each passing year, and living from letter to letter, visit to visit and if for any reason this life-giving communication from the outside is severed it becomes a torture worse than death. It becomes, not living, but a kind of suspended animation in which the meaning of one's existence is sustained through a vicarious process, devoid of normal day to day emotional content.

But I am compelled to thoroughly immerse myself in the prison culture and draw upon it for the necessary emotional and intellectual sustenance I require to fulfill my being. This does not mean that I've totally rejected and forgotten my former life, which is really the primary focus of my existence—I am only *here* temporarily. I have family and friends, memories of the past and hopes for the future that are very dear to me. But I keep them in a separate place within myself, that warm spot I have reserved for my deceased mother and all my childhood memories. It is there that I live and relate to the world outside, I receive and respond to letters and visits with great joy and enthusiasm, drawing strength and inspiration from their love and concern—then turn my attention back to the here and now.

Relationships are difficult to sustain through time and distance, and the strongest of them begin to weaken over the years, until the letters are finally reduced to a ritual of words. They lack the physical presence of human to human contact and the emotional vibrancy that grows from it. Convict relations span the entire human spectrum, from the most casual to the swearing of life or death allegiance. I have found a camaraderie in these relations that have served me well, and there is always someone available to share a problem with, to bitch and complain with, to laugh with, or someone just to sit around the yard and bullshit with. And then there are the special ones with whom I share my secret hopes and fears, who prop me up where I am weak and build me up where I'm torn down. It is through them that I have been able to endure.

However, having such friendships is not without risks, both physically and emotionally. It is easy to become dependent upon a particular individual's presence in your daily affairs, especially after you've become comfortable with his style of doing time. And if he goes home or is suddenly transferred, you are left with an empty hole. Also prison is a violent condition, and if death is stalking your partner, it is most likely on your trail too. So whatever trouble he buys means you are guaranteed a serving, whether you were in on the deal or not. And even if you escape the knife, how do you deal with his death? It is an agonizing dilemma which has driven guys to seek revenge against their comrade's assailant or to protective custody lock up for their own safety, both of which are extremely difficult decisions. For those, and other reasons, it is *safer* to keep all acquaintances on a casual basis, but in doing so you lose the sharing and caring that go into the making of real friendships. As for me, I prefer the risk.

What Does it Mean

I have testified to the truth of my condition as I know and understand it as it is, but I don't know the meaning of this truth.

Does the fact that I've come to terms with my imprisonment mean that I have surrendered my life to it? Or that I've found such a secure haven that I have no need to return to the streets again? Or maybe I'm afraid! Or maybe just lazy! Or maybe stir crazy! I don't know what it means. I suppose I could make an argument to justify my position, but it would be an empty exercise. It means what it means . . . nothing more, nothing less!

My experience with *the prison* has been a long, arduous struggle; it has laid to waste twenty years of my youth, but in these final hours I have learned to live in the existentialism of the moment. At this juncture of my life I am in prison and I am determined to live as fully and completely as its limitations will allow. The success or failure of my life lies in this instant; I have weighed myself in the balance, and claim victory instead of defeat.

BOOKS OF RELATED INTEREST

Penetrating chapters on pleasure, freedom, fear, death, time, the unconscious mind, love, sexuality, meditation, and human evolution make THE PASSIONATE MIND by Joel Kramer an important manual for contemporary living. 128 pages, soft cover, $3.95.

In SELF-ESTEEM/A DECLARATION, therapist Virginia Satir presents an essential credo for the individual in modern society. 64 pages, soft cover, $2.95.

World-renowned family therapist, author, lecturer and consultant Virginia Satir begins a major new series dealing with family roles in MAKING CONTACT. In this initial volume, she brings to a popular audience innovative techniques for improving family communication through learning the essence of making contact. 96 pages, soft cover, $3.95.

In ALPHA BRAIN WAVES, David Boxerman and Aron Spilken analyze the mystery surrounding research into the alpha state and examine the industry that has evolved from it. 128 pages, soft cover, $4.95.

In HOW TO BE SOMEBODY, noted psychologist Yetta Bernhard presents a specific guide for personal growth that will "lead to acceptance of one's self as a human being." 128 pages, soft cover, $3.95.

In SELF-CARE, Yetta Bernhard tells her reader to say "I count," and describes exactly how to put the premises of self-care into practical, everyday living. 252 pages, soft cover, $6.95.

CELESTIAL ARTS
231 Adrian Road, Millbrae, California 94030